THE RIGHT TO REMARRY

By *Dwight Hervey Small*

DESIGN FOR CHRISTIAN MARRIAGE
AFTER YOU'VE SAID I DO
CHRISTIAN: CELEBRATE YOUR SEXUALITY
THE RIGHT TO REMARRY

THE RIGHT TO
REMARRY

DWIGHT HERVEY SMALL

FLEMING H. REVELL COMPANY
Old Tappan, New Jersey

Scripture quotations not otherwise identified are from the Revised Standard Version of the Bible, copyrighted 1946, 1952, ©
1971 and 1973 by the Division of Christian Education of the National Council of Churches, and are used by permission.

Scripture quotations identified NAS are from the New American Standard Bible, Copyright © THE LOCKMAN FOUNDATION 1960, 1962, 1963, 1968, 1971, and are used by permission.

Library of Congress Cataloging in Publication Data

Small, Dwight Hervey.
   The right to remarry.

   Bibliography: p.
   1. Divorce—Biblical teaching. 2. Remarriage.
I. Title.
HQ824.S57   261.8′34′27   75-17655
ISBN 0-8007-0758-3

TO

countless evangelical Christians who have experienced divorce
and remarriage despite every attempt under God to avoid it, and
who have agonized over the scriptural validity of what they have
done. And to those pastors whose conscience and counsel have at
times been at odds with their understanding of Scripture in this
critical matter. To all these, this book is dedicated with the utmost
empathy. May the Spirit of grace and truth lead us into the wider
place, where liberty in Jesus Christ most perfectly matches His
highest will for every expression of redeemed life—including the
marital.

Contents

THE RIGHT TO REMARRY

1

We Need a New Approach

*Pastor, have I the right to remarry? It's been nearly four years
since John decided that he wanted out. I've been seeing a fine
Christian widower and the children feel as I do that we could
reestablish a Christian family. Pastor, have I the right to remarry?*

In one form or another that question repeats itself daily.
Perhaps no more controversial subject haunts the Church than
that of divorce and remarriage. To write on the subject is to
place oneself in the midst of a highly emotionalized, dogmati-
cally controverted debate. For today it is not simply a matter of
academic interest; it touches the lives of countless evangelical
Christians presently either divorced and remarried, or divorced
and alone—usually alone with children.

In one way or another, the Church sees to it that the divorced
cannot forget their peculiar status. To be divorced and unat-
tached is to be an anomaly in the Church, consigned to a most
difficult and untenable position. To be divorced and remarried is
to suffer a less difficult position only because it is a less conspicuous one. If the fact remains unknown, there is no problem.
But the stigma and the strictures are all around. Most commonly, a divorced man cannot serve as the pastor of a church,
although this is changing reluctantly in some quarters. More frequently, it is the lay person who discovers that he or she is no
longer worthy to serve as a church officer or Sunday-school
teacher. It is tacitly recognized that divorce carries a moral

stigma whatever the conditions may be, and this leads to some form of social ostracism.* Strange, but one can be forgiven nearly any other failure known to life and be restored to a place of service within the church—confession and penitence does the trick.* But to be divorced and remarried is to have committed the unpardonable sin for which there is no restoration to service for Christ in the Church.* This book is a protest to all that, a call for an end to this kind of injustice and ecclesiastical immorality! And whether we understand the Scriptures in the light of a presupposition—as some will suggest—or whether the Scriptures do indeed allow for a broader view, will remain the judgment of the reader. The book shall present the case for Redemptive Realism.

To the contemporary evangelical pastor, this has become a perplexing problem by virtue of the growing number of divorced and remarried persons in his congregation, many of whom would qualify as his most committed and gifted Christian men and women. He senses a certain incongruity between the situation as it is in reality and what the Church has consistently taught over the years. The question then arises: Do we have new insights into the ethics of divorce and remarriage, insights developed in the light of today's changing needs and today's greater understanding of scriptural ethics?

In the failure of the Church to provide "a new word," divorced and remarried Christians frequently turn to secular sources for help in the difficult transitions they face. One such book is the best-seller entitled *Creative Divorce*. Surely, if divorce and remarriage are not realistically recognized as a fact of life among Christians, then of course no comparable books may be expected from Christian writers, and there will be little advance in the pastoral ministry to such persons. What pastoral ministry there is will be within the context of viewing divorced persons as exhibits of failure, restorable to emotional, even spiritual health, but not to a normal family pattern nor to full service in the Church. The penalizing aspect will not have been removed; unspoken judgment will continue to be evident.

If we have any indication in the rush of Christians to such books on popular psychology as *I'm OK, You're OK,* perhaps we shall see the same rush to such books on divorce as *I've Had It, You've Had It.* Will the Church then be responsible for turning her people to secular sources in the absence of serious Christian literature that dares to take life as it is found? Will they look in vain for a truly redemptive ministry in the Church of Jesus Christ? Will they stumble over our use of the word *grace?* If in this sphere of personal relationships there is no fully redemptive, restorative possibility for life's failures, there can hardly seem to be redemptive possibilities in other areas either. Redemptive Realism is an all-embracing concept in Scripture, or it is to be questioned altogether.

Today, many Roman Catholic scholars are taking a new look at the Scriptures which touch on this subject. Some creative possibilities are being discussed, as we shall take note further on. The strong dogma of the Church is being intuitively resisted as intrinsically unsatisfying to mind and conscience alike. Little new has emerged from evangelical Protestantism in thirty years. Even a controversial book—as the present book will likely prove to be—perhaps may stir others to enter into dialogue and produce some worthy insights to match the desperate need.

In the realm of biblical ethics, as in the realm of biblical theology generally, there remains a great divide between two systems—Dispensational and non-Dispensational. The complete standoff may be subject to moderation as ethics and eschatology provide areas for interface. Eschatology has become more prominently recognized as the context of Jesus' ministry, and the divorce-remarriage question relates to the eschatology of Jesus and the Kingdom. This book will seek to present both the Dispensational and the non-Dispensational approaches to ethics and eschatology, seeking throughout to show that both approaches are amenable to the final conclusions which are reached. On a more personal level, this book is designed to bring reassurance to divorced-and-remarried Christians, to say to them that God's redeeming and renewing grace reaches to every condition of life, offering possibilities that a zealous legalism has long shut off. May the message of these pages serve to challenge pastors to consider a pastoral ministry more in harmony with the principles of grace which dominate the New Testament Epistles. In brief, this book sees divorce and remarriage as neither a personal nor an absolute individual right. It is permissible at times, not because the Kingdom Law of Christ provides for it, but because the redemptive grace of Christ does not preclude it. Although never God's pure intention, divorce and remarriage nevertheless come within His conditional will for those who face the irreversible reality of marital breakup. The grace of realized forgiveness does not suspend God's absolute ethical demand, but transcends the legal requirements of it in the face of failure. Grace is restorative, not punitive, extending even to the sinful disruption of the marital commitment.

Whenever the question of divorce and remarriage is raised in evangelical circles, the answers conventionally include the following: "Scripture allows no divorce at all," citing Jesus' words in Mark or Luke as final. Or: "Divorce is allowable only in the case of a partner's adultery," citing Jesus' words in Matthew, and sometimes allowing remarriage, sometimes not. Or: "It is permissible only if an unbelieving partner wants it," citing Paul in First Corinthians, and with some granting remarriage while others do not. Within the limits of these answers is found the characteristic response of evangelical Christianity up to and including our day. Consensus is hard to come by, as responsible scholars differ.

A problem of this magnitude and with such serious implications for the pastoral ministry, ought to send evangelicals back to the presuppositions of their theology to at least *search* for the possibility of a broader ethical context. It is a rare pastor's conference on marriage and family life that doesn't surface the agonizing doubts of pastors who must minister to divorced people, and who have serious questions as to how they might harmonize the words of Jesus—which seem so totally restrictive and unbending—with the ethic of the Epistles—which seems to emphasize God's gracious forgiveness for all sin and failure. For in this larger New Testament ethic, they do not find the inclination to categorize or penalize those who fail in areas other than in marital experience. And of all places where penalty is most severe and socially damaging—having its most profound effect—marriage and family is that place. I, as a professor of marriage and family studies in a Christian college, face untold numbers of students who struggle with what seems contradictory to them—the approach of the Synoptic Gospels as viewed against the approach of the Epistles. They find *law* in the Gospels and *grace and realized forgiveness* in the Epistles. They ask, "In what sense, if any, has Jesus placed us under a new law?"

Utmost care must be taken to deal with this subject so that the impression is not gained that divorce can be taken lightly. As Dominic Crossan says, "The bond of marriage is privileged in law because it is sacred for life. It confines and protects the family as the primary community of love. The inherent durability of the marital union is necessary for the realization of the basic values of civilized society, and so it has been sustained in all nations by the rule of law." God's original intent, expressed in the orders of Creation in Genesis, envisions marriage as indissoluble. It is an exclusive contract of life-partnership, embracing the union of two persons in their totality. Marriage means integration of persons and a surcease to loneliness. Complementarity makes of the marital union something more than the mere addition of two lives. The couple is "one flesh," an expression meant to speak of a total union of persons in mind, body, and spirit. But when marriage fails to become a catalyst for human personality, the normal road to full self-realization, then marriage as intended does not exist, despite whatever other characteristics of marriage may be present.* Or when marriage creates and sustains loneliness, and supplants integration of persons with disintegration, it is bereft of its essential meaning. While two people may continue to live alongside each other, enacting all the familiar marital rituals, the marriage itself may be dead. In Christian faith, the exemplarity of God's love for man is symbolized in marriage, but when the very opposite of such love is a present reality, marriage does not in fact exist at all. No formal contractual recognition can make of this a marriage; internal divorce has already taken place and simply awaits formal recognition.* The fidelity, the love, the self-sacrifice, and devotion of husband and wife to each other and their children are meant to speak more clearly than words of Christ's love for the Church. But when this is nonexistent, then marriage as intended does not exist and it becomes difficult, if not impossible, to talk about what God has joined together.

Absolute prohibition of divorce, or prohibition except for the cause of adultery, no longer commands the adherence of many responsible scholars. Quite frankly, the debate in theological ethics is moving in another direction, and this book is a serious call for pastors and counselors to get with it—for sound biblical reasons, at that! We recognize that some pastors will resist any new or seemingly unconventional approach all the way. Others are simply fearful because of the entrenched bias on this subject which characterizes much of evangelical Christianity. Conventional teaching is sacrosanct: only theological liberals will tamper with it! *Beware! Beware! Any treatment of divorce which seems to make it more acceptable can only be regarded as an evil which will further contribute to the breakdown of our day.* Equally prevalent, however, is the pastoral acknowledgment that while the head says one thing, the heart says another. The stringent demand made by Jesus somehow seems out of keeping with the nature of God's grace and realized forgiveness. The idea of a lifelong penalty in the area of man's most basic need —for mate and home—seems incongruous. We have trouble with this command, similar to the trouble we have with the radicalized demands of the Sermon on the Mount. The death of marriage among sincere and growing Christians is sometimes undeniably final, yet the acknowledgment of that fact is often denied in the refusal to recognize the possibility of divorce or to permit remarriage following divorce. A solution to this problem must be found not only in a supportable interpretation of the meaning of words and phrases found on the lips of Jesus or Paul, but also—and perhaps more basically—in the vision of New Testament morality as a whole.

This book is written to provide an alternative to the evangelical *party line* on divorce and remarriage, better described as the *hard line*. That position claims to be biblical; so equally does the alternative position. Whereas the traditional evangelical position is content to provide an impeccable exegesis of the particular New Testament passages, the alternative position undertakes to view divorce and remarriage in a larger light than can be gained from particular passages where the subject is under discussion. It is in the light of theological ethics, contextual in approach —not content to see relevant passages in isolation. This is the key to it all. There is a progress of ethical contexts revealed in Scripture, so that not every ethical saying applies to all; not every ethical declaration can be universalized. The will of God, unchanging in itself, is administered differently in different periods in His relationship with mankind. The most obvious illustration of this is the mere mention of the Old Testament administration of Mosaic Law—from which New Testament believers are set free. No longer, for example, are we commanded to stone to death those who are guilty of adultery. Rather, we seek to lead them to saving grace and realized forgiveness in Christ. Much of the confusion relating to the sayings of Jesus has to do with the fact that He often spoke as One who stood firmly within the Mosaic Law, time and again relating what He said to this particular ethical context. So much of what we read in the Epistles is notably absent from the words of Jesus, for the evident reason that He spoke in the context of the Old Covenant waiting to be fulfilled in His death and resurrection. There the principle of grace apart from works-righteousness was not operative. Nor could the new principles of grace be understood until Jesus had effected redemption, ascended to the Father's right hand, and sent the Holy Spirit to be the indwelling light and power for the new life in Christ. How confusing, for example, to teach a person the way of salvation by grace alone, as outlined in the Epistles, or in the Gospel of John, then quote Jesus' words from the Synoptic Gospels, ". . . unless your righteousness exceeds that of the scribes and Pharisees, you will never enter the kingdom of heaven" (Matthew 5:20).

How, then, does one square New Testament principles of grace and realized forgiveness with the severe prohibitions of Jesus during His earthly ministry? How can one feel right about proclaiming the free and full pardon of *all* sin and failure, while insisting that one failure alone—marital failure—must be forever penalized? Is divorce following the death of marriage really socially unpardonable and unrestorable to the extent that all divorced persons cannot again contract a normal marriage, never enjoy another life-partner, never live normally in the intimate society called the family, never again hold office, or serve significantly in the Church of our gracious Redeemer?

The status of divorced Christians remains unique in the evangelical world, dissimilar to the status of all other Christians who acknowledge equally serious ethical failures in their lives, who admit to less than perfect sanctification. And the reason for this widely disparate categorization? Simply and solely because Jesus spoke of divorce in absolute terms of prohibition and condemnation. Those words, uttered within the contexts of the

Synoptic Gospels and singularly in First Corinthians in the Epistles, are taken as final authority in the matter. The conclusion seems so self-evident as to require no further investigation, and precludes any question of viable alternatives. It is in protest to this comfortable position—this scriptural fixation—that this book is written.

The radicalized, absolute form of ethics in the Sermon on the Mount, which incidentally is nowhere repeated in the Epistles, should prompt the Bible student to ask how this relates to the ethics of grace in the post-Calvary, post-Pentecostal Church. Where are realized forgiveness and new redemptive possibilities. in the Sermon on the Mount? Was Jesus talking to the Christian community, or to His Jewish hearers who stood on Old Testament ground, or in different ways to both? In what way is the Kingdom ethic applied to the present age? Why is it that the most notable feature of Jesus' ethic in the Sermon on the Mount does not go beyond a works-righteousness? Why the total absence of any redemptive aspect in view of the anticipated failure to meet the demands of such an ethic? Is this a new law —imposed upon those whom Jesus was even then soon to lead out from the bondage of the law of Moses? Or is this in fact *law* for the coming Kingdom, but a nonlegal, ethical *ideal* for the present age of grace? Is there a basic modification of terms for the Church Age? These are a few of the necessary questions which must be answered before one can approach the question of divorce and remarriage more directly and ultimately. Before anything else, there must be established the context in which God proclaims His unconditional, pure will. This must be clearly distinguished from the situation in which He acts upon His conditioned will. When and why the Great Transition from unconditional to conditional will? What are the real possibilities for fulfilling God's will for those who live redeemed lives, but live them under the conditions of the fallen aeon prior to the coming of the Kingdom?

The extraordinary feature of God's redemptive work in Christ is that He freely offers pardon to all who come to Him in faith. The utter joy of being pardoned is that one is fully and forever freed from two things: guilt and penalty! But if God does not give divorced Christians reason for continuing guilt, *the evangelical Church most likely will!* If God does not exact a penalty, *the Church in many instances does!* Perhaps even more seriously, where one is the victim of divorce, or where divorce is solely the result of failure—not particular sin—the Church too eagerly treats it as though it were the result of sin. In the most demanding intimate relationship possible, the Church asks for success on the part of every couple, despite the evident fact that with respect to no ethical absolute of our Lord can the Church produce a community claiming such success. Thus it becomes a problem of the Church's unreal expectation. Idealistically, the Church proclaims the sufficiency of Christ and the power of the Holy Spirit for all human problems, and this sufficiency no true Christian would deny. But it is equally true that the power of God is sufficient to heal all who are afflicted physically or emotionally and to secure jobs and income for all who stand in such need. But realism forces us to come to terms with the limitations of Christian believers to appropriate the resources in God. And the mystery remains as to why God does not answer the faith and intercession of all who seek healing, all who need jobs, all whose children are outside the faith, all who cannot make marriage what it is intended to be. The question of God's sufficiency is not the relevant question; it is man's ability to appropriate the sufficiency of God's resources that is at issue. And here we are concerned with the state of individual Christian growth and maturity, the teaching and counsel available, the extremity of conditions debilitating the relationship, and so forth.

No seasoned pastor is unaware of marriages that are impossible, many having been impossible from the day of their beginning. There are, unfortunately, pastors who choose to believe that some people should remain in such impossible marriages regardless of the damage done to themselves and to their children—as though this were God's best for them, and as though God places the formal contractual relationship of marriage above the lives of those who are presently in a destructive relationship. Was marriage made for man, or man for marriage? Is God bound to certain laws which render compassion and grace and release impossible? Is His grace nullified by His law? Or is His law sometimes nullified by His grace? This is the major question. But perhaps we should not suggest that His law can be nullified, even for the sake of making a point. His law can be rendered inoperable in a given situation by the action of His grace; it is not nullified, nor compromised in any way. Nor is His law anything other than absolute. He does not operate on a principle of tolerance, or leniency; He is activated by grace and grace alone. In His redemptive program, mercy and grace supersede works-righteousness. Regardless of that which conditions God's will in the past or the future, Redemptive Realism governs His will for the present.

One thing this book shall not attempt, nor is it appropriate: We shall not concern ourselves with the history of interpretation. Widely divergent views have characterized the Church from the start. For example, the Anabaptist tradition sees the Sermon on the Mount as a radical call to literal obedience, possible for all Christians now. At the other extreme, some Dispensationalists have gone so far as to suggest that the Sermon on the Mount is intended solely for the Kingdom which is yet in the future, having no application whatever to Christians in this age. It will be our major purpose to address this issue squarely and thoroughly. This book takes a definite position with reference to these matters. It does no good to say to people hurting in the midst of divorce that there are half a dozen prominent views on the subject—so take your choice! Anyone who writes on divorce and remarriage places himself in the midst of controversy, and this the author is not reluctant to do, for he has arrived at a position which is not altogether unique, although it seems not to have been extensively developed elsewhere. It is a position which reflects much that is current in theological ethics today. And since the book is written for the average Christian lay person who wants biblical guidelines, it will not be our method to always cite biblical authorities or to credit sources. This book is meant as a very present help in trouble for thousands who have suffered enough without having to suffer the citation of biblical authorities, too! In the last analysis, the value of this study will depend upon the blessing of God upon it.

The author is persuaded from his participation in scores of pastors' conferences and marriage workshops in churches across the land, that the dark shroud we hang on all divorce is largely of our own making. We take the position we want to take, or feel our church body takes, and for very mixed reasons. Rightly do we abhor divorce as such, and the more notorious causes for it. We hate the consequences which follow in the wake of many divorces. We hardly know how to register our compassion for the divorced in any really practical way, for we cannot seem to offer them what they need most—assurance of our hope that they will find a mate and a restored home life. We know that many cannot truly cope with the loneliness of a life suddenly severed (much more difficult after one has known marriage), or possibly with strong sexual needs suddenly rendered nonfulfillable. We all too frequently let the divorced feel themselves to be the unintegrated people at Christian social gatherings, or look upon them with suspicion as though they must surely be predatory creatures with eyes only for the husband or wife of another. Somehow the principle of liberating grace doesn't reach out to the divorced in the same way that Jesus reached out to the woman taken in adultery as recorded in John 8:1–11. He cited the law to her, but acted in grace; forgiveness for her was full and free. No penalties were announced to this sinful woman, no marital restrictions placed against her because of her adultery. She was free indeed! Free because forgiven!

The position taken in this book is as follows: The biblical right of divorce and remarriage is neither a personal nor an absolute right. In fact, it is not a right at all. Such a right is not inherent in the orders of Creation which speak of indissoluble marriage as God's intent. Such a right was granted under the Mosaic Law as a concession of God's grace and conditional will. In the teachings of Jesus which touched upon questions of Mosaic Law, He indicated that the concession was not intended to continue in the Kingdom Age which was to come, except for the cause of unchastity. Then remarriage for either party is tantamount to ethical adultery, for it is a violation of God's absolute intent. But when we look at the larger context of New Testament ethics, beyond the teaching of Jesus directed to the Jewish authorities of His day, we find only one divorce passage in all the New Testament Epistles. This is to the problem-oriented church at Corinth. What Paul teaches there is in answer to their questions, and seemingly he does not go beyond their questions. In fact, he does not seem to go beyond their particular circumstances. And notably, the emphasis throughout the chapter is guided by Paul's grave concern for "the present distress" (*see* 1 Corinthians 7:26). This foreboding condition qualifies all that Paul has to say about singleness and marriage. To say the least, this is negative and restrictive to a degree not found elsewhere in Paul or in any other New Testament writer. Except for the Corinthian passage which gives abnormal counsel for abnormal times and conditions, the Epistles are silent. We shall have to ask ourselves why this is; why is there so little revealed about a matter of such magnitude?

A major portion of our study shall deal with the question of God's will. We shall be speaking of His absolute and unconditional will, and we also shall be referring to His conditional will in terms of His accommodation to human weakness and failure.

In three great ages of God's ethical administration, His conditional will is in force, although in varying ways. During the Mosaic period it was law without the indwelling presence of the Holy Spirit as a divine Enabler. Jesus announced the law of the Kingdom which, because it was rejected, is yet future. Kingdom Law is elevated above Mosaic Law to more perfectly fulfill righteousness. It incorporates internal elements, and the Kingdom Age finds God's people indwelt by the Enabler, the Holy Spirit. But the interim Church Age is administered not by Kingdom Law, but by grace. Thus we shall be making distinctions which enable us to understand how to apply the divorce passages both primarily and secondarily.

Divorce and remarriage, although never God's pure intention, are nonetheless within His conditional will for the redeemed who continue to live under the conditions of the fallen aeon which still prevail in our world. This is nothing less than a divine concession within God's overarching purpose of realized forgiveness. After all, the very ongoing existence of a fallen world reflects the conditional will of God enacted toward mankind. Redemptive grace adapts itself to the failures of the redeemed people of God. The major task of this book, then, is to draw out the implications for people caught today in the inevitability of divorce, perhaps with the hope of remarriage, yet wanting God's sure direction.

After reviewing the available literature on the biblical view of divorce and remarriage—meager to be sure—it seems that evangelical pastors and divorced members of their congregations need a full-length study which goes into the ethical contexts of the New Testament, not content simply to interpret the relevant passages. With Heinrich Baltensweiler we can say, "Nowhere in the New Testament is there a full teaching on marriage. This means that we are not justified in systematically coordinating the relevant statements; instead each statement on marriage must be considered on its own merits and examined in its historical context." Such a study, to be fair to all the necessary considerations, must be true to God's original intent for marriage, while at the same time aware of the larger ethical context of grace that embraces the whole of New Testament ethics. It does not take extraordinary perception to see that many of the words of Jesus in the Synoptic Gospels stand in tension with the ethical principles of grace in the remainder of the New Testament. Classically, evangelicals in the past have resolved this tension by simply resorting to the words of Jesus without attending to the contexts in which they are found. Impeccable exegesis of individual passages, however, fails in the end if the contextual material is not thoroughly determined as well. Thus the traditional studies on divorce and remarriage have been dogmatic, incredibly circumscribed, generally forcing Jesus' words into the ultimate teaching of the New Testament.

More liberal scholars, while rightly sensing that the ultimate ethical direction of the New Testament is not legalistic nor judgmental, have tended toward a resolution of the tension by relegating Jesus' teaching to an earlier statement, more primitive because of its close association with the Mosaic milieu, but amended by the mature idealism of later New Testament teaching. In such an approach we have a compromising of Jesus' words without really resolving the tension. This latter approach is neither biblical nor necessary. Instead, the tension is to be retained between the absolute words of Jesus and the ethical context of grace in the Epistles, and in the relationship between the two there emerges a principle which satisfies a thoroughly Christian understanding. The absolute gives form to God's pure and original intent—His absolute, uncompromised righteousness. Grace gives form to God's present enactment of His conditional will on behalf of human weakness and failure, to accommodate His will to weakness and need.

One of the major problems to be faced in this study is to distinguish the contexts of law—both Mosaic and Kingdom—which dominate the Synoptic Gospels (Matthew, Mark, and Luke), from the totally different ethical context of the fourth Gospel, John. It must be apparent to the most superficial student that John's Gospel is harmonious in its message and orientation with the Epistles, while the Synoptic Gospels contain a Kingdom message which is all but foreign to the remainder of the New Testament, the Book of Acts excepted. Jesus' ministry to Israel—and only to Israel—is in full evidence in the Synoptic Gospels and in the early chapters of Acts. The transition from *Israel under the law* to the *Church under grace* took place over a prolonged period which dates early in Jesus' ministry and runs on through the period covered by the Book of Acts. This period ended historically with the destruction of Jerusalem and the turning of the apostles to the Gentiles. That this transition did not take place all at once is traceable in the ethical teachings of the New Testament. In terms of this transition, it shall be noted that the words of Jesus relating to divorce and remarriage come in the early period when His message was directed to Israel. This must be kept in mind if we are to seek to correlate this precisely with the Christian ethic.

The very idea of such a transition may be new to some readers. *Isn't the Church the same as the Kingdom?* No, it is not indeed. Nor is the Church building the Kingdom. This was the message of Protestant liberalism for decades, but it is far from supported in the Scriptures. The residual effects of this view remain, however, and it is curious to see Christians thinking they are able perfectly to fulfill the Kingdom Law as represented in the Sermon on the Mount. Those who try, hardly know what to do with the judgments also expressed in the Sermon on the Mount, for inevitable failure then means judgment, not grace! But for those who need further evidence for what we have called the Great Transition, consider the words of Jesus in Mark 2:19–22 where the scribes and Pharisees ask Jesus why His disciples do not fast. His reply is that the old dispensation is now passing away and the new is coming in. According to Matthew 11:13 (also Luke 16:16), the prophets and the law ceased with John the Baptist, while John's Gospel tells us: "For the law was given by Moses, but grace and truth came by Jesus Christ" (*see* John 1:17). So the transition began long before Pentecost, although Pentecost was a climactic and pivotal point in the process of transition, for there the Holy Spirit descended to baptize believers into the Body of Christ, and to indwell believers. His indwelling presence changes the degree of response which believers are able to make to the ethical demands of God.

The key to it all is the rejection of the King and Kingdom which occurred during the entire period of Jesus' ministry, coming to its climax with the entry into Jerusalem and the official rejection which took place there. Since, however, His offer of the Kingdom was a bona fide offer, Kingdom teaching dominates the major portion of the Synoptic Gospels. Much of what Jesus concerned Himself with during this transition was the Mosaic Law and its proper interpretation. He internalized the demands of the law to show what true righteousness required, and He more thoroughly absolutized that law when He spoke of the requirements of the Kingdom which was then "at hand," and which now is still to come. But intermingled with these teachings which relate either to the Mosaic Law then passing, or the Kingdom Law, much of which is yet in abeyance, is a preparation for the Church Age. Features of this transition can be noted all the way throughout the Book of Acts, if one is curious to look for them. For remember, the destruction of Jerusalem and the Jewish Temple did not take place until A.D. 70, a rather extended time following the resurrection of Christ nearly forty years earlier. God's judgment upon the nation was delayed for the very special reason of giving that generation of Israel another opportunity to repent and to turn to Christ. The national chastisement of Israel and dispersion from the land did not take place until this opportunity had been given. This shows that God was still dealing with Israel until well into the beginning of the Church Age. Ethically, there is evidence of the same gradualism in the shift from the old administration of Mosaic Law to the new administration of the Church under grace. This cannot be ignored in the ethical placement of Jesus' sayings on the subject of divorce and remarriage.

The third ethical context to which the New Testament draws our attention is that of the coming Kingdom. It is to be consummated with the return of Jesus the King. It is to be that time when the redeemed shall occupy their resurrection bodies, a time when Satan's power shall be bound. Obviously, a higher ethical context will prevail during that Kingdom Age. Yet, sin will not have been eradicated until the final great cataclysm. God will continue to administer His will in a conditional way. The absolute ethical requirements of a holy God will then be *enforced,* even as now they are *declared.* The King shall rule in righteousness—righteousness far more absolutized than is now possible. Until then, we live as Christians in an ethical interim, in partial sanctification and with degrees of failure, yet ever being renewed and restored by redemptive grace.

We must be careful to acknowledge, as Dispensationalists often do not, that the Kingdom *did* briefly appear in the Person of the King. Its righteousness was glimpsed in the few and brief references to the Kingdom ethic. In the Sermon on the Mount there was a foregleam of that ethic. But if the Mosaic legislation had been impossible of fulfillment under the conditions of man's fallenness, so shall the Kingdom ethic—radicalized by Jesus—be impossible of fulfillment under the conditions of the fallen aeon by which we live today. This does not suggest that we have no relation to the Kingdom ethic, however. In it we are given to understand the ultimate righteousness of God, and we are to set these requirements as our own ethical ideal. As the goal of Christian living, we can seek, by the power of the Holy Spirit, to conform as nearly as possible. Yet it shall be the "impossible possibility," as others call it. The ideal is as high as God Himself, "Be perfect as your Father in heaven is perfect" (*see* Matthew 5:48). No less an ideal could ever be appropriate for a people of God governed in righteousness. Yet in view of the inability of His people to perfectly achieve the ideal, the administration of God's will for this interim Church Age becomes that of grace and realized forgiveness. To understand this is not to attempt to make the Kingdom ethic a new law, binding upon Christian believers. It was never intended to be that: Christians possess it as an ethical demand, a guide for Christian life, but subject to failure and renewing grace.

Now, of course, this book will not present an acceptable alternative to those who insist that the Church Age is synonymous with the Kingdom, who do not distinguish the different ethical contexts in the New Testament. Nor will it be acceptable to those who hold to the possibility of holiness perfected in this life. But to those who hold to the futurity of the Kingdom and its absolute ethic, who perceive the present interim period as the Church's age of grace, not law, this study should represent a coherent development. To the present writer, the burden of the New Testament Epistles is that the redeemed are positionally sanctified in Christ, but they live out their lives under the conditions of an imperfect sanctification which at best is progressive. Although redeemed, not every area of daily life is redeemed. No one is perfectly mature in his growth in holiness and Christlikeness. Each is a sinning and failing creature, ever subject to the need for forgiveness, cleansing, and the renewing grace of God in Christ. How clear this is in 1 John 1:7–9, in Romans 7, and in Galatians 5!

A final preliminary note concerns a principle prominent in this study. The biblical student must distinguish particular historical contexts which have their limited application, from those contexts in which principles are intended to have universal application. Nowhere is this more important, for example, than when

we turn to 1 Corinthians 7, the one passage on divorce and remarriage in the New Testament outside the Synoptic Gospels.

The ultimate consideration of this book will be an attempt to
place the whole question of divorce and remarriage in the light
of Redemptive Realism. The immediate task, in contrast to the
long-range one, is to pursue the themes introduced in this first
chapter. It is a necessary journey if we are to be truly contextual. For those who may be a bit impatient with the journey, a
glance at the final chapter is always permissible, for there the
conclusion of the matter is finally reached, and some practical
words are addressed to pastors in particular. The final words are
affirmative of the triumph of grace over all sin and failure, and
the liberty of those who are set free by Jesus Christ to live their
broken lives in the new possibilities of Redemptive Realism.

So let it be said once more before we begin our journey: This
is far more than a book on divorce and remarriage. It is a book
about New Testament ethics, and especially how we must dis-
criminate between the ethics of the Mosaic Law, the ethics of
the coming Kingdom, and the ethics of the present age of grace.
Divorce and remarriage cannot even be discussed until this ethical system is properly oriented. Only then will we return to the
subject of divorce and remarriage, for only then will we be prepared to see just how to interpret the words of Jesus in what
shall be referred to as a secondary application. The impact of
the whole message of this book depends upon first studying the
New Testament as a Book with more than one ethical context.
So stick with it, and the reward will come at the end!

2

Old Testament Origins

Quite naturally we turn first to the Old Testament for the origins of biblical teaching on divorce and remarriage. What we find there is meager, somewhat obscure, and largely incidental. There is no systematic teaching on the subject; it seems virtually of no concern to the Old Testament to pursue the themes of monogamous marriage, marital disruption and divorce, or the consequences of remarriage. The *Encyclopedia Judaica* says that divorce and remarriage were accepted as an established custom in ancient Israel. This assumption clearly lies behind the few references in the New Testament. The subject of divorce really does not appear at all until the Mosaic legislation is given. In fact, there is no marriage law as such, so there can be no contravening of marriage law by divorce. Marriage is not set in legal or contractual terms, but rather is based on a principle which was noted at the very first union of man and woman. Immediately following the creation of Eve and her union with Adam, we read in Genesis 2:24: "Therefore a man leaves his father and his mother and cleaves to his wife, and they become one flesh." The Creation orders are suited to mankind before the Fall. Marriage was designed to be indissoluble, an enduring relationship through life. A growing unity was to characterize marriage so as to make it a total union of persons in a common life. The concept of *one flesh* brought together all the components of personal life. Marriage was a complementary union in which both husband and wife were completed by the other. Life became an integrated whole whenever a man and a woman were permanently united. Marriage made an organic whole of which the two persons were equal complementary halves. Without the forces of evil to disrupt this union, Adam and Eve represented the ideal of marriage without possibility of divorce. No provision for divorce and remarriage was made a valid part of the orders of Creation. It was to this that Jesus referred in Matthew 19:8: ". . . but from the beginning it was not so." He pointed to God's original intention, an intention which had not changed. No divorce or remarriage had been programmed for mankind's marital experience under the conditions of original sinlessness. Only the disruption and disorder of a fallen world could make this a necessary option for mankind. The rupture of this divinely instituted human bond is conceivable only if first of all there is a rupture in the divine-human relation. At the very outset this enunciates the nature and basis of marriage and clearly implies that no dissolution of the marriage bond could be contemplated except as a radical breach of the divine institution. It was impossible to envision any marital dissolution as anything other than abnormal and evil. Such was the ethical context of "the beginning" when mankind was as yet free from the thralldom of sin.

With the entrance of sin came a new complex of conditions and circumstances. Since sin desecrates all relationships, we are bound to face the question of the bearing of sin upon the sanctity of marriage. With failure and disruption generally permeating human relationships, it was inevitable that such failure would manifest itself in the most intimate and demanding of life's personal relationships—marriage. Granting the original principle of the indissolubility of the marriage bond, are there now, by reason of sin, conditions under which marriage may be dissolved with divine sanction and authorization? Shall the intention of God be conditioned by the necessities of man's weakness and failure? John Murray reflects, "It is quite conceivable that while the reason for divorce is sinful, the right of divorce for that reason may be divine.''

By the time the nation Israel was organized around Mosaic Law, divorce and remarriage had become customary practice. Israel was little different from her neighboring nations in this respect.

From the Pentateuch we are unable to discover that God instituted a divorce law. It is also true that God did not institute a law prohibiting divorce. We must acknowledge that if divorce were to be regarded as an absolute prohibition among God's people, Israel, it must be assumed that a divine law of prohibition would have been incorporated within the Mosaic legislation. Especially is this to be expected when it is seen that there are restrictions placed on divorce and remarriage in the law. In some cases divorce was forbidden, in other cases it was mandatory. From the standpoint of God's intention, divorce and remarriage were concessions to man's weakness and failure. Interestingly, there is no biblical example of divorce being invoked by holy men of God. Divorce is always a regrettable necessity when it occurs.

To understand that divorce was an absolute dissolution, the term *to cut off* was used to indicate complete severance. The bill of divorcement was referred to as ''A Bill of Cutting Off.'' The New Testament Greek employed a word equivalent to the Hebrew. The Hebrew word also means ''to put away,'' and is translated thus in some versions. Interestingly, when in the opening pages of the New Testament we read that Joseph suspected Mary of infidelity because she was pregnant with the Holy Child, we read: ''. . . being a just man and unwilling to put her to shame, resolved to divorce her quietly'' (Matthew 1:19). In the King James Version the more literal rendering is ''to put her away.'' Here also is tacit admission of the right of private divorcing. As a just man, Joseph had that right.

Coming now to the Mosaic Law as it related to divorce, we

refer especially to the study by David Amram. In the Mosaic Law as detailed in Deuteronomy, there were two laws restricting the husband's right to divorce, and one that refers to that right. Deuteronomy 21:10–14 refers to the woman taken captive at war. She may be taken as a wife. If, however, the husband finds no delight in her in time, he may let her go where she will. She is privately divorced. Deuteronomy 22:13–19 has to do with the husband who falsely accuses his wife of prenuptial incontinence. His punishment is to be deprived of his right of divorce; he is compelled to keep her as his wife forever. Further on in the same chapter (vv. 28, 29) is a second and similar law, by which punishment is prescribed for the man who rapes a woman. He must marry her, pay a sum to her father for the violation of his daughter, and he shall never be permitted to divorce her all of his days.

Now, before the enactment of these laws the husband was under no restriction whatever, and could divorce his wife whenever he pleased. By these laws his liberty received its first check. The right of divorce had been a private right of husbands, the natural outgrowth of the patriarchal system. The woman was never entitled to divorce her husband under Jewish law. Such an act would have been in opposition to the rights of the husband over the wife. The idea of a bill of divorce given by the wife to the husband was quite impossible to the Jewish legal mind.

The legal and social status of the divorced woman is scarcely touched upon in the Bible. There is nothing to indicate that her position was in any sense an inferior one, but, on the contrary, she seems to have enjoyed certain advantages denied to married women. The divorced woman, like the widow, was her own person. She could return to her father's house, but she need not. Before her marriage the woman was subject to the authority of her father; during the marriage her husband was her master; if widowed or divorced, she did not once again become subject to her father's authority. She then had the right to give herself in marriage, whereas as a maiden, before her maturity, she was given in marriage by her father. Unlike an unmarried woman or a wife, she could bind herself by her vows (Numbers 30:10). The only absolute disadvantage that a bill of divorce imposed upon a woman was the denial of her right to marry a priest (Leviticus 21:7). Lest it appear from this passage that a divorced woman is classed in bad society, Philo says, "They [the priests] are permitted with impunity to marry not only maidens, but widows also; not indeed all widows, but those whose husbands are dead, for the law thinks it fitting to remove all quarrels and disputes from the life of the priest; and if they have husbands living, there very likely might be disputes from the jealousy which is caused by the love of men for women; but when the first husband is dead, then with him the hostility which could be felt towards the second husband dies also." Philo is speaking of women who are widowed by divorce, a curious use of the word to us, but his point is clear.

The High Priest of Israel, by virtue of his exalted and sanctified position, was not permitted to marry a woman other than a virgin. Spiritual symbolism is to be found in the Prophets especially where one speaks of Israel as the one wife of Jehovah. Paul uses the same terminology when he speaks of bringing the Corinthians to Christ, ". . . I betrothed you to Christ to present you as a pure bride to her one husband" (2 Corinthians 11:2). Other versions translate: "pure virgin" or "chaste virgin." The restriction placed upon the High Priest goes further than that placed upon the marriage of a priest, for the High Priest may not marry a widow. So the widow is placed in the same class as the divorced woman. It is not that divorce downgrades a woman or a priest who should marry a divorced woman. We must be careful to note that the whole point is symbolic of a spiritual truth; the priest is to represent God's pure intention of being the Husband to a virgin people. Spiritually, this speaks of an enduring marriage of God and His people, a marriage not incorporating the idea of marital disruption and complexity of husbands. Later in the Prophets, Israel is pictured as the unfaithful wife and God separated from her for a season. The marriage is reestablished with the repentance of God's chosen people. His covenant with Israel shall stand despite even the unfaithfulness of that people.

The form of the bill of divorce mentioned in Deuteronomy, and the formalities attending its delivery are obscure. Our conception of it dates from much later times. By analogy to known forms of legal procedure of very ancient times, it has been supposed that the giving of the bill of divorce was a formal act, done in the presence of the elders, similar to the practice mentioned in Deuteronomy 22.

Anticipating the counsel of the Apostle Paul to the Corinthian church regarding the problem of unbelieving spouses and his permission for Christian husbands or wives to let them divorce if they want, we can look with interest at the mandatory nature of divorce in the special circumstance that confronted Ezra and Nehemiah during the reform movement of their time. The account is found in Ezra 10 and Nehemiah 13, and is best expressed in the words of Shecaniah to Ezra:

> We have broken faith with our God and have married foreign women from the peoples of the land, but even now there is hope for Israel in spite of this. Therefore let us make a covenant with our God to put away all these wives and their children, according to the counsel of my lord and of those who tremble at the commandment of our God; and let it be done according to the law.
>
> Ezra 10:2, 3

God had forbidden marriage with these people, so to divorce these wives was to repudiate their sin. In the New Testament we are told (in 2 Corinthians 6:14) not to yoke ourselves together with unbelievers (the Revised Standard Version reads "mismated"). However, the word to Christians who find themselves married to unbelievers is that they should not for that reason divorce their mates. This must be the decision of the non-Christian spouse, if it is a decision at all (*see* 1 Corinthians 7:12–17). Comparison of the Old and New Testament passages is indicative of the vast difference between the divine administration of law and grace. Divorce is never mandatory in the New Testament, nor is it ever commended; at best it is permitted as "a regulation of necessity," to use the words of Helmut Thielicke. It is only in the sphere of grace, never in the sphere of law, that we can speak of "the lesser of two evils." Grace can manage this concept, law cannot. The Old Testament saint was not left to make the "tragic moral choice," but the New Testament saint is. In the sphere of grace, conflicting values must at times be weighed and a discriminating, difficult choice made. How much greater is the difficulty of decision in the sphere of grace, how searching the motivation of the one making such decisions! Yet under the governance of grace, the good of the individual or couple is more than a mere matter of legal arrangement.

We turn now to the most important Old Testament text —Deuteronomy 24:1–4—a passage that occupies a unique place in the Old Testament because it contains, as does no other passage in the Old Testament, specific legislation bearing upon the question of divorce. But to say this is also to point out that it is not a legal text for divorcing; like other texts, it takes divorce for granted. This is to say that legislation very likely did exist, but it was not included in the Pentateuch for some reason difficult to understand. Perhaps it existed in oral tradition. But it is a legal text nonetheless, the purpose of which is clearly regulative. Thus it is improper to speak of it as a "concession." It is not that either, strictly speaking; it is regulative law within the Mosaic corpus of law. No better summary statement is available than that of S. R. Driver, "The law is thus not, properly speaking, a law of divorce; the right of divorce is assumed, as established by custom . . . but definite formalities are prescribed

and restrictions imposed, tending to prevent its being lightly or
rashly exercised." This passage in Deuteronomy has special
significance which is confirmed by references to it in both Testaments.

> When a man takes a wife and marries her, if then she find no
> favor in his eyes because he has found some indecency in her,
> and he writes her a bill of divorce and puts it in her hand and
> sends her out of his house, and she departs out of his house, and
> if she goes and becomes another man's wife, and the latter hus-
> band dislikes her and writes her a bill of divorce and puts it in her
> hand and sends her out of his house, or if the latter husband dies,
> who took her to be his wife, then her former husband, who sent
> her away, may not take her again to be his wife, after she has
> been defiled; for that is an abomination before the Lord, and you
> shall not bring guilt upon the land which the Lord your God gives
> you for an inheritance.
>
> Deuteronomy 24:1–4

This is the only legal text which refers in any detail to the
termination of marriage by way of divorce. Reuven Yaron points
out that nothing in the text in any way expresses disapproval of
divorce. It is certainly conceded to be the status quo, and there
is no civil or ecclesiastical ostracism attached to it. On the contrary, it is legal and fully effective in giving the wife the right of
remarriage. One reason for the legislation is that it aims to prevent hasty divorce on the part of an angry husband. After all,
divorce was utterly simple to obtain; there were no court cases.
The ease by which it could be obtained required a tempering
influence. This regulative law provided just that. Yet this cannot
be the major reason. At the time when a husband divorces his
wife, he is not likely to take into account the legal situation
which will arise after the dissolution of a subsequent marriage of
his wife some years hence. Yaron sees this as protecting the
second marriage. When the divorced wife has married another,
we have the possibility of tension. The first husband may wish
to get back his wife, and if she remarried in haste, she, too, may

wish to return to her former husband. She may draw comparisons and want her first husband back if he will take her. Such a situation could also cause the second husband to go through the pain of jealousy and apprehension. But all these possibilities are avoided once such a reunion with the first husband is precluded by law. The concern of this passage is not an objection to a second marriage, but rather to take effective steps to ensure its stability and continuation. Instead of refusing to allow divorce, it makes sure that divorce will stick! It also seeks to ensure that the remarriage will stick.

Related to this text in Deuteronomy is the analogy drawn in Jeremiah 3:1: "If a man divorces his wife and she goes from him and becomes another man's wife, will he return to her? Would not that land be greatly polluted? You have played the harlot with many lovers; and would you return to me? says the Lord." The argument of the prophet is this: If a man cannot have his former wife back after one additional lover, how much more will Israel be unable to return to God after having had many lovers. The Prophet Isaiah carries forward the concept of God as Husband:

> For your Maker is your husband, the Lord of hosts is his name . . . . For the Lord has called you like a wife forsaken and grieved in spirit, like a wife of youth when she is cast off, says your God. For a brief moment I forsook you, but with great compassion I will gather you.
>
> Isaiah 54:5–7

The thought is that of God's love never permitting Him to put away His people. There may be a temporary separation, but not rejection. From Hosea on, the prophets represent the indissoluble bond between God and His people as a marriage relation, founded on God's unchangeable love.

Upon the return of the Israelites from captivity in Babylon, some of them divorced their Jewish wives in order to marry the heathen women among whom they had taken up their residence in Palestine, whom they otherwise would have had to leave behind. It was a cruel and wanton use of divorce. Against this abuse Malachi raised his voice. The law was powerless to prevent this divorcing, but morality could not countenance it. Malachi says that this is why God will not answer their prayers:

> You ask, "Why does he not?" Because the Lord was witness to the covenant between you and the wife of your youth, to whom you have been faithless, though she is your companion and your wife by covenant. Has not the one God made and sustained for us the spirit of life? And what does he desire? Godly offspring. So take heed to yourselves, and let none be faithless to the wife of his youth. "For I hate divorce, says the Lord the God of Israel . . . . So take heed to yourselves and do not be faithless."
>
> Malachi 2:14–16

What God hates is this treacherous putting away. We must not generalize from this that He hates all instances of divorce. But when faithlessness leads one to divorce—God hates that divorce. We must keep this in context and not make it apply to every case. What God hates is the nonfulfillment of His design for marriage, whatever the cause, as it may render divorce inevitable.

Now, back to our passage in Deuteronomy 24 once again. The crucial yet controversial part of the text has to do with the words, ". . . she finds no favor in his eyes because he has found some indecency in her . . . and the latter husband dislikes her." What ambiguous words are these for a legal text! The versions are of little help here. The King James Version reads "some uncleanness," New American Standard Bible, "some indecency," while the Jerusalem Bible has "some impropriety." The Living Bible, apparently unable to come to anything precise at all, simply says, "If a man doesn't like something about his wife . . . ." The Hebrew literally says, "the nakedness of the matter," but this is idiomatic and gives no clue at all to the English reader. The phrase is variously interpreted in the Jewish Talmud, differing in time and place. In the Torah and Masoretic text it is translated "unseemly" and "obnoxious." This ambiguity has resulted in a wide division of thought as to just what the Scripture means, and the practical effects have been most unfortunate, for it opened the door to every kind of abuse.

In the first century before Christ, the rabbinic schools of Shammai and of Hillel were locked in controversy over the meaning of this term. The school of Shammai interpreted nearly all the biblical laws strictly and rigorously. They held that only sexual immorality was cause for divorce. This doctrine was completely at variance with the customary right of the husband. The school of Hillel, on the other hand, was generally more liberal, holding that the husband need not assign any reason whatever for his divorce action since anything which displeased him to the extent of desiring to divorce his wife was adequate cause. One hundred years later the question was still the subject of debate, although the ancient tradition, supported by Hillel, seems to have prevailed. A commanding authority of that time, Rabbi Aquiba, held with the school of Hillel. The same opinion was held by Philo of Alexandria, one of the most distinguished philosophers and jurists of his time. The noted historian, Flavius Josephus, shared this view, writing, "He who desires to be divorced from his wife for any cause whatever, and many such causes happen among men, let him in writing give assurance that he no longer wishes to live with her as his wife." And the article in the *Encyclopedia Judaica* of our time endorses the opinion of Hillel in interpreting the phrase to mean any kind of obnoxious behavior or mannerism.

John Murray deduces that the following facts bear most cogently against the view that this means adultery: (1) The Pentateuch prescribes death for adultery (Leviticus 20:10; Deuteronomy 22:22–27). (2) Numbers 5:11–31 provides for cases of suspected adultery, but the penalty is not divorce—nor does

it apply to charges of sexual uncleanness against a newly wed-
ded wife. Deuteronomy 22:13–29 deals with this condition, but
not through divorce. (3) The law provides for all kinds of con-
tingencies in the matter of sexual uncleanness, but in none of
these cases does this phrase occur, and in no case is there recourse to divorce.

What are we to say? Two things impress themselves upon us:
First, our expectation is that in matters of legal prescription and
proscription the most precise, unambiguous language will be
employed. This certainly is to be expected with regard to the
divine law given by God and recorded under the inspiration of
the Holy Spirit. Second, the history of interpretation leaves no
question that the crucial phrase in this text is ambiguous. To the
writer this suggests one thing. There is a divine reason which
justifies ambiguity in this legal reference. Even our Lord did not
take the opportunity to clear up the controversy when He was
asked pointedly what was meant. His response was to say that
the divorce permission was granted because of "your hardness
of heart" (Matthew 19:8). He left the causes in the realm of
ambiguity, coming down with great force to add, "And I say to
you: whoever divorces his wife, except for unchastity, and marries another, commits adultery" (v. 9). In the next chapter we
shall consider at greater detail what Jesus meant, and in what
context. Suffice it to say here that, all things considered, the
Mosaic Law assumed the right of divorce as a regulation of
necessity, and attached little importance to the formalities. Its
chief concern was a protective one so far as the wife was concerned, and to inhibit impulsive divorce on the part of the
husband—purely practical concerns. As for justifiable cause for
divorce, the law seems deliberately ambiguous, leaving it a matter of personal judgment and not in any sense a matter for the
court. There were no civil or ecclesiastical penalties attaching to
divorce, and no question whatever but that divorce allowed remarriage. The process as it came to be a matter of custom was a

very simple one. The husband had to write out the bill of divorce in the words prescribed and return his wife's dowry. The words of the bill read as follows: *Let this be from me your writ of divorce and letter of dismissal and deed of liberation, that you may marry whatsoever man you will.*

Under the most rigorous system of Mosaic Law, divorce and remarriage were gracious concessions of God for a most difficult problem in the most intimate of personal relationships, marriage. The question then naturally arises: Will there be a more or a less rigorous law of divorce and remarriage in the New Testament? Or will there be, perhaps, a more rigorous law in terms of the righteousness demanded in the Kingdom, but a more gracious rule in view of human weakness and failure during the Church interim of grace? The latter is the presupposition which finds confirmation in this book.

We conclude this brief look at the Old Testament with the simple additional note that the Mosaic permission of divorce was not ideal but remedial. This in itself is an exhibition of God's caring grace, and that the lesser of two evils must sometimes prevail. In a fallen world inevitably there will be a conflict of values where at times the tragic moral choice must be made.

3

The Kingdom Setting

An observation which most writers on the subject of divorce and remarriage seem to miss is that the recorded words of Jesus are found in the midst of His teachings concerning the Kingdom. The Kingdom known both to the Old and New Testaments is the Kingdom covenanted by God to the nation Israel, His chosen people. The continuity of the Old and New Testaments lies in the Kingdom which was prophesied in the Psalms and Prophets of the Old Testament, and offered by the King who came and was rejected in the New Testament. Whether or not that Kingdom takes on a partial fulfillment in the Church which exists during His absence, this Kingdom was irrevocably covenanted with Israel. Its rejection means that its full appearance and establishment on earth is delayed, postponed until certain conditions are effected which once again make its coming possible.

In the interim, the Kingdom is present in mystery form and even its ethical norms must be qualified to be adaptable to the interim. Upon the rejection of its King, Israel as a nation has been set aside for a time. During the interim period before the King returns to establish His Kingdom, God is not redemptively inactive; rather, He is doing a new thing among mankind. He is establishing His Church, a body of believers who received Jesus as their Saviour and Lord and who are united to Him in His spiritual presence. The inscripturated Word of God is their external guide, the indwelling Holy Spirit their inward Guide. Although the Church manifests the reality of the Kingdom in a partial way, the Church is not the Kingdom. New Testament believers are members of that Kingdom and will participate in its consummation which is yet future. That earthly Kingdom will occupy a period of time, will have its own distinct history on earth in the same manner in which the Church has its own distinct history on earth.

As the Kingdom is not to be confused with the Church, neither is it to be confused with the eternal state. The Kingdom on earth will be the vindication of all God's earthly purposes, so long frustrated by the sin of man. But that Kingdom, although characterized by peace and righteousness under the rule of the King, will nonetheless be marked by the presence of unregenerate mankind. There is a developmental aspect in the establishment of Christ's perfect rule. This will necessitate the rule of law; the Kingdom will be an ordered society externally controlled by Kingdom Law. The lawful conditions for a rule of righteousness and peace will be enhanced by the presence of the King, the binding of Satan's power, and the presence of the redeemed of the Church Age. It is for these reasons that the Kingdom Law will be an intensified form of law, suitable to the higher possibilities of human fulfillment beyond that which is to be expected in the Church Age.

It is a glimpse of this Kingdom Law that we have in the ministry of Jesus during the period when the chief burden of His ministry was the offer of the Kingdom to Israel. Just how the Kingdom Law, given for the conditions of the consummated Kingdom, is to be adapted and qualified for the conditions of the Church living in the Old Aeon is the problem tackled in this book. How does this adaptation and qualification affect the matter of divorce and remarriage? After all, the question was legislated very differently under the Mosaic Law, yet this, too, was a preform of the Kingdom. The fundamental problem with virtually every study on divorce and remarriage known to the author is the failure to distinguish the different ethical contexts of

Scripture, to deal with the necessary transitions from one to another, and to find the proper qualification of transitional ethics. For example, to introduce Kingdom Law improperly into the nonlegal ethical system which consistently characterizes the New Testament Epistles, is to hopelessly intermingle two vastly different ethical approaches. Law and grace are intimately related, but not to be equated. There are significant differences between the ethical system of grace and the ethical system of the Kingdom, which is eschatological and to be consummated in the future, just as there are significant ethical differences between the system of grace and the ethical system of the Kingdom as Israel knew it under Mosaic Law.

The major denominations of our day, which have built their theological systems upon the teachings of the Reformers, have by and large attempted to equate the Church and the Kingdom, denying an eschatological Kingdom in literal fulfillment of the Old Testament prophecies to Israel. The result, quite naturally, has been to regard Kingdom ethics as a kind of new law for the Church. The Kingdom is completely spiritualized and directly adapted to the life of the Church, without any qualification. Jesus is simply charged with a misplaced eschatological vision. The Kingdom has not been seen as that which is to be consummated in the future, and which has broken through in partial, conditioned fulfillment. Today, the eschatological Kingdom of the end-time is recognized more readily, although only Dispensationalists see in it the irrevocable covenants with Israel literally fulfilled. For the purposes of this book, the ethical considerations are equally applicable to the Dispensational and non-Dispensational understanding.

The same problem is faced whenever there is failure to see that the Sermon on the Mount has an eschatological setting, that its first, primary applications are sometimes to the future Kingdom. To attempt a direct, unqualified application to Christian life in the Church interim is to invite serious contradictions. This is why Reinhold Niebuhr, standing in the interim, could say, "The ethic demands an absolute obedience to the will of God without consideration of those consequences of moral action which must be the concern of any prudential ethic . . . ." We must also recognize that the elevated examples of Kingdom Law which Jesus gave are only examples; they are samples of Kingdom Law, not a full legislation. So it is that we must give careful consideration to the time and circumstances—*when* He said *what* He said, and *to whom*. Transitional aspects must be especially noticed. Utmost care must be given to noting when God's purposes are conditioned by man's response, and when God chooses optional ways because human response has necessitated either His immediate judgment or the operation of His grace in the choice of an option. It is for these fundamental reasons that our study of divorce and remarriage must involve a clear understanding of the setting in which Jesus' words are found, and a sure determination as to the way the Kingdom ethic may or may not be applied to those members of the Kingdom who must live out their lives prior to the coming of that Kingdom with its special ethical conditions. In what ways has God provided a unique ethical system for those living during the interim Church Age? Just what do we mean by the ethics of grace and realized forgiveness? In what special ways is the will of God administered conditionally to those believers living under the circumstances of the Old Aeon?

Our first observation is that the three Synoptic Gospels—Matthew, Mark, and Luke—link the New Testament with the Old Testament. They form an historical transition in which many dominating concerns are Old Testament concerns. That which has come must relate to that which was prophesied, and this is the burden of the Synoptic Gospels and the Book of Acts. This is not the burden of John's Gospel or the Epistles. The Synoptic Gospels form that important bridge. They answer such questions as: Is there a fulfillment of Israel's expectations? Is

this the King and the Kingdom so long anticipated? What are the
credentials? What is now required for its establishment? Should
it be rejected by Israel, will there yet be an eschatological consummation? Would there then be a preform, partial fulfillment
during the interim? Would there be a transitional form of Kingdom ethics? If so, in what exact particulars?

The major message of the Psalms and Prophets is the anticipation of an earthly Kingdom with God's Messiah reigning and
ruling. Israel, God's chosen people, waited with longing for the
arrival of One who would inaugurate the Messianic Kingdom in
accordance with irrevocable, divinely promised covenants.

Although the expression *the Kingdom of God* does not occur
in the Old Testament, the idea is found throughout the Prophets.
God is spoken of as the King, both of Israel and of all the earth.
Although He is now the King, it is also said that He shall become King and shall rule over His people. God's rule is therefore something realized in Israel's history, however partially and
imperfectly. The Prophets look forward to a day when God's
rule will be fully expressed, not by Israel alone, but by all the
world. The Old Testament word *malkuth* is used both for the
reign of a king and the realm over which he reigns. There is
nothing incongruous about this; they are the two inseparable
parts of a single complex idea, as Eldon Ladd has demonstrated,
along with many others.

God, who visited Israel in Egypt to make them His people,
and who has visited them again and again in their unique history
as His people, must finally come to them in the future to judge
wickedness and to establish His Kingdom. It was and continues
to be an eschatological hope. The Kingdom will see the rise of a
Davidic King who will rule over a restored Israel, bringing peace
to all the earth and drawing all nations under God's perfect rule.
This hope, which could only be introduced by suprahistorical
forces—by the direct act of God—is firmly rooted in the pre-
exilic prophets.

The earth has been involved in the evils which sin has incurred; therefore the earth must also share in God's final redemption, that His glory may be then perfectly manifested in His Creation. The curse which lies upon nature because of man's sin precludes earth from being the scene of the final realization of God's Kingdom apart from a radical transformation; this will take place in the end-time. The new age of the Kingdom will be so different as to constitute a new order of things. Isaiah, for one, saw that new order in terms of a new earth (Isaiah 65:17; 66:22). The Prophets look forward to the deliverance of the whole Creation from "the bondage of corruption" (*see* Isaiah 11:9; Romans 8:21).

God called Israel to be the people of His rule; He entered into irrevocable covenants with them. Their failure and judgment cannot cancel out God's victory or reverse His covenants, for that would be allowing the failure of man to also bring about the failure of God and His promises. That Israel's failure may bring about a postponement of their national relation to the Kingdom, a delay in the final consummation, and an interim preform of the Kingdom is altogether feasible. This, in fact, is what occurred. After Sinai, God's sovereignty was manifested in Israel; the theocratic nation experienced the Kingdom of God by obedience to the Mosaic Law.

Eschatologically, "in the latter days," Isaiah sees the final era of righteousness and peace (Isaiah 2:2 ff.). *In the latter days,* Israel will turn to the Lord and David, their king (Hosea 3:5). *In the latter days,* Israel will be restored, only to be assailed by the evil hosts of Gog (Ezekiel 38:16). "The days are coming" when God will restore the fortunes of Israel with security and blessing (Amos 9:13 ff.). *The days are coming* when a righteous Branch will spring forth from David to execute justice and righteousness; Judah will be saved and Jerusalem will dwell securely (Jeremiah 33:16). And so many irrevocable promises are given to Israel.

Now, this Day of the Lord for the prophets was both an immediate act of God expected in history and the ultimate eschatological visitation. The prophets did not usually distinguish between these two aspects, but viewed them as though they were one. This is suggestive of the manner in which the New Testament student must distinguish the coming eschatological Kingdom in its full consummation, and the preform of the Kingdom manifested presently in the world through the Church. Similarly, the distinguishing characteristics of the Kingdom ethic as they are applicable to the present, and differently applicable to the future, must be recognized.

The Old Testament picture is not of man freely pardoned by God, freely forgiven his sins, Psalm 51 and other passages notwithstanding; it is a picture of one who must have works-righteousness after the legislation of the Mosaic Law. Righteousness was obedience to the law as it externally applied. Jesus startled the Jewish authorities by insisting that true righteousness includes freedom from anger, lust, retaliation (Matthew 5:21–48). And yet Jesus did more than promise the forgiveness of sins; He bestowed it. He did more than assure men of the future fellowship of the Kingdom—He invited them into fellowship with Himself as the present King of that Kingdom. He did more than promise them vindication in the day of judgment—He bestowed upon them a present righteousness.

Thus it is that Jesus came as a Jew to the Jewish people, accepted the full authority of the Mosaic Law during His ministry, conformed to Temple practices, engaged in synagogue worship, and throughout His life lived as a Jew. He took His stand squarely within the background of the Old Testament covenant and the promises of the prophets. He recognized Israel, to whom the covenant and the promises had been given, as the natural "sons of the Kingdom" (Matthew 8:12). His mission was to proclaim to Israel that God was now fulfilling His promises and was to bring Israel to its true destiny. Because Israel was the chosen people of God, the age of fulfillment was offered not to the world at large but to the sons of the covenant.

New Testament scholars generally agree today that the burden of Jesus' message, as recorded in the Synoptic Gospels, was the Kingdom. William Barclay comments that "Matthew's dominating idea is the idea of Jesus as King." There is growing consensus that the Kingdom of God is in some sense both present and future. We concur with Eldon Ladd that the tension between the future and the present is the tension between the Kingdom in complete consummation and the Kingdom in process of breaking in upon the present order in partial but genuine fulfillment.

The only Scripture available at first to the early church was the Old Testament, which during the period of time covered by the early chapters of Acts would only accentuate to a largely Jewish church the Kingdom expectations with which they were completely familiar. For many aspects of Kingdom teaching, the Old Testament was the one and only court of appeal so far as divine revelation was concerned. Early New Testament preaching in the Apostolic Church was tested by its agreement with the Old Testament writings. Recall the Berean Jews who were commended because, after hearing Paul, ". . . they received the word with all eagerness, examining the scriptures daily to see if these things were so" (Acts 17:11). It certainly seems that our Lord and the apostles assumed that the Old Testament Scriptures were sufficiently understood as to make their hearers responsible for believing the message which they brought, a message which in every way shared a continuity with their Old Testament. For, although the burden of Jesus' message was the Kingdom of God, He nowhere defined it. Nor is it recorded that anyone asked Him what "the Kingdom of God" meant. He assumed that this was a concept so familiar in its entirety that it did not require definition.

Misunderstanding prevails wherever there is failure to discern

that four of the historical books of the New Testament seem
clearly to have as their major message the connection of the Old
Testament promises of Israel's Kingdom with their fulfillment in
Christ—whether in relation to His First Coming or Second.
These four New Testament books are not the four Gospels;
rather they are Matthew, Mark, Luke, and Acts. John's Gospel
is for the most part in a different category. He does not deal
with the transition from the Kingdom offered and rejected to the
Kingdom postponed and present in unique partial manifestation.
His concern is with the redemptive truth and life which more
directly relate to the Church in the interim. But the three Synoptic Gospels and Acts all deal with the transition from the initial
offer of the Kingdom to Israel to the establishment of the
Church for this time. The first Kingdom offer is recorded in the
Synoptic Gospels, the second in the Book of Acts. All of this is
simply stated at this point in our study; the scriptural evidence
will follow as we proceed.

There is a twofold character to the ministry and teaching of
Christ during the time between the inauguration of His public
ministry and the cross. This is recorded with uneven emphasis
in the Gospel accounts. He came as a minister to Israel to
confirm the promises made to the fathers, and He came as a
minister to the Gentiles—the entire non-Jewish world—that they
might glorify God in His mercy to those outside the promises
(Romans 15:7–9). The problem with many students has been the
failure to distinguish these two ministries as separate but related. They are intermingled in the text of the Gospels, and must
be identified by the character of the message and the circumstances under which they are found. To some extent there is a
comingling of the teachings of grace principles for living in the
Synoptic Gospels, but this is indeed a far less developed theme
within the broader context of Kingdom teachings. It is to be
remembered that these teachings recorded in the Synoptics were
given while the law of Moses was in full continuing effect. Jesus

lived and taught under the authority of the Mosaic Law, and that economy prevailed until His death and resurrection. There is in these Gospels some anticipation of the age of grace, but it is little more than anticipation, for grace principles are not explicitly taught until we come to the Epistles and to the Gospel of John. This has no important reference to chronology of writing, but to the subject matter and purpose for writing. Jesus' recognition of the Mosaic system is everywhere present in His teaching. The Gospels thus reveal their complexity, since they are a composite of the teachings of Moses, of the coming eschatological Kingdom, of the Kingdom as it is in process of breaking through, and a glimpse of the principles of grace. The various sayings of Jesus cannot be taken with simple directness as though everything He said were addressed unqualifiedly to us.

The teachings of Jesus, confirming the covenants with Israel, and offering the Kingdom under certain conditions, are found almost altogether in the Synoptic Gospels. This accounts for the long tradition in the Church to regard the position of the Gospels among the New Testament books as appropriate. They follow immediately upon the Old Testament, which closed with its great hopes unrealized and its great prophecies unfulfilled. These hopes were based on irrevocable covenants which God had made with Israel. These covenants guaranteed to the nation Israel an earthly Kingdom under the reign of Messiah. He was to sit on the throne of His father, David. When Christ came into the world, no such promise had been fulfilled, no such Kingdom existed.

The first ministry of Jesus was to Israel as her long-expected King. There was nothing in this ministry to reveal Him as a personal Saviour who would sacrifice Himself for sin. He appeared as Israel's Messianic King, the One with the right to David's throne. In the Synoptic Gospels there was therefore no record of any movement toward the formation of the Church, or any reference to that great purpose at all, until His rejection as Messiah had been irrevocably established. The role of the Twelve as the incipient Church was not disclosed until that time. Nor was His return to earth ever mentioned until after His rejection was evident. It was after this that Jesus related the fulfillment of every covenant promise to Israel with His return. The Kingdom promises, unfulfilled because of the rejection of the King, remain unfulfilled to this hour. But they are not set aside. They will yet be fulfilled when the King returns. In covenant faithfulness, God will bring to consummation every promise relating to the throne, the Kingdom, and the nation.

During the days of His ministry to the nation Israel, Jesus endorsed the Mosaic legislation, but not the interpretation of it made by the scribes and the Pharisees. At the same time He spoke of the new principles which were to be applied in the Kingdom as "these sayings of mine." It was not until the Upper Room Discourse that He used the term *my commandments*. At that time He unfolded the new principles which were to govern the daily living of those who belong to the New Creation under grace. Notably, this discourse is found in John's Gospel, not the Synoptics. John 13:34 is the first use of the term *commandment* in the message of grace. So far as its use in the Synoptics is concerned, it is the period after His resurrection when He says, "Teaching them to observe all that I have commanded you" (*see* Matthew 28:20). This includes, of course, what is recorded earlier. But it is not a generalization which in any way obviates the fact that what He taught must be understood in its proper ethical contexts, applied in accordance with our understanding of the Kingdom partially fulfillable at present, perfectly fulfillable at the eschatological consummation.

We shall see that when the Kingdom was rejected and its consummation delayed until the return of the King, so was the special application of all teaching which conditions life in that future Kingdom delayed as well. That application in its unqualified form shall be delayed so long as the King is absent, inasmuch as it can be applied only when there are Kingdom conditions supportive of its fulfillment in the lives of its royal subjects. That there are similarities between Kingdom teachings and grace teachings is fully to be expected, yet this fact does not constitute law and grace as an indivisible whole. It remains the task of responsible students not to confuse the two systems. Application of Kingdom righteousness is most surely made to the Church, but in ways other than unqualified legalism.

The New Testament opens with one message: the announcement of Israel's Kingdom now at hand. It was spoken to Zechariah, the Virgin Mary, Joseph, and the shepherds (*see* Luke 1:11–17, 26–35; 2:8–15; Matthew 1:20–25). It was anticipated by the Magi, celebrated by Elizabeth, and in Mary's Magnificat, also by Zechariah's prophetic utterance (*see* Matthew 2:1–6; Luke 1:39–79). This announcement of the Kingdom is called *gospel* or good news in Mark 1:14, and is to be distinguished from the *gospel of saving grace* in later New Testament disclosures. This good news was preached first by John the Baptist, later by our Lord Himself, then by the Twelve, and last by the appointed Seventy (*see* Matthew 3:1, 2; 4:17; 10:5–7; Luke 10:1, 9, 11).

That Israel's great hope was still expected at the time Jesus appeared is expressly declared in Luke where the angel announces to Mary:

> And behold, you will conceive in your womb and bear a son, and you shall call his name Jesus. He will be great, and will be called the Son of the Most High; and the Lord God will give to him the throne of his father David, and he will reign over the house of Jacob for ever; and of his kingdom there will be no end.
>
> Luke 1:31–33

Frederick Godet, with whom we concur, says of this: "The throne of David should not be taken here as the emblem of the throne of God, nor the house of Jacob as a figurative designation of the Church. These expressions in the mouth of the angel keep their natural and literal sense. It is, indeed, the theocratic royalty and the Israelitish people, neither more nor less, that are in question here; Mary could have understood these expressions in no other way. It is true that, for the promise to be *realized* in this sense, Israel must have consented to welcome Jesus as their Messiah . . . . The unbelief of Israel foiled this plan, and subverted the regular course of history; so that at the present day the fulfillment of these promises is still postponed to the future."

The Synoptics uniformly present Jesus as the King of this Kingdom. The very first recorded word about Him concerns His descent from the royal line of Israel: "The book of the genealogy of Jesus Christ, the son of David, the son of Abraham" (Matthew 1:1). To emphasize His kingly claim, Matthew actually reverses the historical sequence, naming David before Abraham. Take the Magi who came asking, "Where is he who has been born king of the Jews?" (Matthew 2:2). Herod himself inquired where the Messianic King would be born, for this was a threatening feature of Jesus' birth to him. The answer was harmonious with prophetic remembrance: ". . . in Bethlehem of Judea, for so it is written by the prophet" (Matthew 2:5). Both Mary and Joseph were descendants of the royal house of David, Joseph through the legal line of Solomon, Mary through the line of Nathan (Matthew 21:2–16; Luke 3:23–38). Early in His ministry, Nathanael expresses his faith by saying, ". . . you are the Son of God! You are the King of Israel!" (John 1:49). The very term *Christ* is the Greek equivalent of the Hebrew *Messiah,* applied in the Old Testament prophecy to the Messiah-King of Israel.

Early in the Synoptic Gospel accounts, the announcement of the Kingdom was authenticated by miraculous works. Jesus also gave authority to perform miracles to the Twelve, whom He sent to announce the good news of the Kingdom (Matthew 10:1–8). Later the same authority was given to the Seventy who were appointed to precede Him. As they went, they were to say,

". . . the Kingdom of God has come near to you" (Luke 10:9). And even after His entry into Jerusalem in royal manner, miracles were given to authenticate His claim before the chief priests. The long-awaited Kingdom of Old Testament prophecy had indeed come so near to that generation of Israel that they had actually seen the face of the King, and had witnesssed the supernatural works which were the predicted harbingers of His Kingdom. And this Kingdom is either essentially the same as that predicted by the prophets, or it is not. No evidence exists to suppose that Jesus entertained any concept of the Kingdom other than that predicted. To spiritualize this Kingdom is thus to do violence to an enormous body of Scripture, both Old and New Testament. It is thus that we must keep distinct the future, end-time Kingdom, and that Kingdom partially breaking through in the spiritual presence of Jesus in the Church interim.

Absence of any formal description of the Kingdom in its initial announcement indicates that the Jewish hearers were expected to know exactly what the Kingdom was all about. The announcement simply concerned the fact that its time had come (*see* Matthew 3:1, 2; 4:17; Mark 1:14, 15). The one other significant aspect which was new was that national repentance was a necessary condition on their part.

Jesus never intimated that His conception of the Kingdom differed either in kind or degree from that prophesied by the Old Testament prophets. He explicitly said that He had come, not to destroy the prophets, but to fulfill them (Matthew 5:17). As our Lord began His preaching in Nazareth, He first identified Himself, then justified His ministry in their midst, from a prophetic passage in Isaiah (*see* Luke 4:7–21). He read from the last section of Isaiah's prophecies which have to do with God's anointed One who will bring in the promised Kingdom. Later, when He took up His Galilean ministry, Matthew 4:14–16 connects it with a prophecy in Isaiah 9:1, 2, which is best known for its context and the inclusion of the words: "Of the increase of his government and of peace there will be no end, upon the throne of David, and over his kingdom, to establish it, and to uphold it with justice and with righteousness from this time forth and for evermore . . ." (Isaiah 9:7).

Later in His Galilean ministry, Jesus was asked why His disciples did not fast. He replied that this would be incongruous "as long as the bridegroom is with them" (Matthew 9:15). This idea of the divine Bridegroom was not unfamiliar to Jewish hearers, for it held a central place in the prophetic Scriptures concerning Israel in the days of the coming Kingdom (Isaiah 61 and 62). In that Kingdom, Israel will again be married to the Lord (Hosea 2:19, 20). Betrothal shall be forever; this covenant promise shall not fail. (Note Hosea 3:4, 5 for a prophetic indication of the interim when Israel will not have a king.) And make no mistake, Jesus identified Himself as the Bridegroom spoken of in the Old Testament. How gloriously this truth is amplified in Isaiah, chapter 54!

The primacy of Israel in Jesus' ministry is reflected in His word to the Gentile woman. He had refused to respond to her plea on behalf of her daughter, saying, "I was sent only to the lost sheep of the house of Israel" (Matthew 15:24). Again, when He commissioned the Twelve, it was with the strict command, "Go nowhere among the Gentiles, and enter no town of the Samaritans, but go rather to the lost sheep of the house of Israel" (Matthew 10:5, 6). Surely, no one will say that the Twelve thought at that juncture that the Kingdom for Israel was not to come to pass, and that they were instead the incipient Church! They had one message: "And preach as you go, saying, 'The kingdom of heaven is at hand' " (v. 7).

The fulfillment of Israel's covenants may very well be interrupted temporarily as a temporal judgment against the nation. However, the divine promises shall never be abrogated, or God is untrue to His word. There is to be a future restoration, a truth made known to the Church through the Apostle Paul (Romans

11:11–15). There shall be a rebirth of the nation (Isaiah 66:5–13). Hosea forecast this, too. God had pronounced judgment upon a wicked Israel, only to say immediately: "Yet the number of the people of Israel shall be like the sand of the sea, which can be neither measured nor numbered; and in the place where it was said to them, 'You are not my people,' it shall be said to them, 'Sons of the living God.' " (Hosea 1:10). In the next chapter, God says, ". . . I will say to Not my people, 'You are my people'; and he shall say, 'Thou art my God.' " (Hosea 2:23). The Kingdom, taken away from the present rejecting nation, shall incorporate them in a primary way in the consummation. Repentant and regenerated, a spiritually new nation shall exist at that future time, a witness to God's covenant faithfulness and redeeming power and grace! This was God's specific, irrevocable promise to Israel.

The Kingdom was "at hand" because the King had arrived and was in their midst. There could be no Kingdom established on earth without such a King present. It follows, therefore, that to reject the King is to reject the Kingdom. The initial announcement carried the necessary contingency: "The time is fulfilled, and the kingdom of God is at hand; repent, and believe in the gospel" (Mark 1:15). The "gospel," or good news, that they were to believe was the good news of the King's arrival; it was not the gospel of salvation through the sacrifice of God the Son.

Unrelentingly, opposition built between official Israel and her appointed King. The crisis came, strikingly, when Jesus cast out a demon from a man both dumb and blind. The Pharisees acknowledged the miracle but attributed it to the power of Satan (Matthew 12:24). It was bad enough to reject Christ as a lawbreaker, which they had recently done (John 5:16), but now to charge Him with doing the miraculous by the power of Satan, was infinitely worse. For now they are ascribing wickedness to their own Messiah, and this provoked Jesus to say:

> Every kingdom divided against itself is laid waste, and no city or
> house divided against itself will stand; and if Satan casts out
> Satan, he is divided against himself; how then will his kingdom
> stand? And if I cast out demons by Beelzebul, by whom do your
> sons cast them out? . . . But if it is by the Spirit of God that I
> cast out demons, then the kingdom of God has come upon you.
>
> Matthew 12:25–28

Jesus' final judgment upon Israel's official response is declared
in verse 32: ". . . whoever speaks against the Holy Spirit will
not be forgiven, either in this age or in the age to come." The
issue had been drawn, the conclusion reached. The evidence
was before the eyes of all. Israel had rejected her King! The
corporate responsibility of the nation was indicated when, four
times in the following discourse, Jesus pinpointed the responsibility of "this generation" for His rejection. For individual Jews
making that evil choice there shall be no restoration to the covenant privileges. For the nation Israel there was the specific
specter of temporal judgment, climaxing in A.D. 70, within the
time span of that same generation. Jerusalem, Israel's capital
city, along with the Temple which represented all of Israel's
spiritual privileges, was destroyed. The nation was scattered in a
worldwide dispersion which was to endure for centuries—until
1948, as a matter of fact.

Malachi, the last of the Old Testament prophets, had predicted the appearance of Elijah as the precursor of the Kingdom
(Malachi 4:5, 6). And Jesus had declared concerning John the
Baptist, His own precursor: "And if you are willing to accept it,
he is Elijah who is to come" (Matthew 11:14). Jesus referred to
John again, this time after Israel's decision to reject Him: "Elijah does come, and he is to restore all things" (Matthew 17:11).
However, while this remains true of the future events surrounding the coming Kingdom, there is a paradox—the King has already come, and preceding Him came one in the character of a
precursor: "I tell you that Elijah has already come, and they did

not know him . . ." (Matthew 17:12). This was a clear reference to John the Baptist. Here is a strong indication of the nature of prophecy's partial fulfillment at the First Coming of Christ, its complete fulfillment in abeyance until the Second Coming.

From this point on, Christ's ministry is of the nature of preparation for the interim, the period of His absence from earth physically—the Church Age which precedes His coming again. It is very apparent from the narrative that a wholly new epoch in our Lord's ministry had now begun. In this ministry His death and His Second Coming are prominently mentioned. The purpose of His teaching now is to prepare the disciples for the interim between His ascension and His return in glory to establish His Kingdom. He turns to parables, whose purpose is to reveal truth to the disciples—and the Church of which they shall be incipient members—at the same time concealing that truth from the rejecting nation. To the disciples He says, "To you it has been given to know the secrets of the kingdom of heaven, but to them it has not been given" (Matthew 13:11). This turning point was earlier prophesied in Isaiah 6:9, 10. These secrets of the Kingdom concern truth not revealed in the past, and not revealed now to a rejecting people. But to His disciples, this is important truth relating to the interim.

The mystery of the Kingdom is the coming of the King into history in advance of its apocalyptic manifestation. It is partial fulfillment, not consummation. This is the single truth illustrated by the several parables in Matthew 13 (also Mark 4). The Kingdom which is to come in apocalyptic power in the end-time has in fact entered into the world in a hidden form to work secretly among men. This was an utterly novel idea, for the Old Testament gave no such promise nor intimation. This present aspect of the Kingdom in mystery form does not replace the expected eschatological Kingdom, nor reinterpret it; it does not supplant but supplements it. This new thing is the Church.

The setting for Jesus' startling announcement concerning the Church which He is to build, is the occasion of His disciples' return from their mission to announce the nearness of the Kingdom. ". . . Who do men say that the Son of man is?" (Matthew 16:13). This self-chosen title *Son of man* derives from Daniel's great prophecy of Messiah and His Kingdom (Daniel 7:13, 14). The disciples report many answers to that question, but not that anyone had confessed Jesus to be the Messiah. Then the question is addressed to the disciples themselves, followed by Peter's magnificent confession, "You are the Christ, the Son of the living God" (Matthew 16:16). It is at this strategic moment that Jesus announces the coming formation of the Church (v. 18). We cannot emphasize sufficiently the importance of this turning point in the ministry of Jesus!

There had been no preconditioning of the disciples for this new thing. The Church was not something that could have been considered legitimately so long as the imminent establishment of the eschatological Kingdom was a possibility. The Church exists only because there was a postponement of the eschatological Kingdom, and thus an interim form of God's believing community. This is not to suggest, however, that the Church was not in the predetermined plan of God.

Now that the historical moment had arrived, when the rejection of the Kingdom was an accomplished fact beyond all dispute, Jesus announced the Church—not as something He had been building all along, or was then building, but was to build. And although the Church is not the Kingdom, to the Church was given the "keys of the kingdom of heaven" (Matthew 16:19). A specifically ordained authority is given to the Church for its time, relating it directly to the Kingdom in a preform of the eschatological Kingdom. Both the future and the present are encompassed. The Church has a preparatory role to play, and those who are brought to salvation are members of the Kingdom to come, yet experience the Kingdom as it is present in advance. The life of the King is theirs by the Holy Spirit, the word of the

King is theirs by the written Word, and the powers of the King are theirs. The Church does manifest the Kingdom in a partial fulfillment of the Messianic ministry.

Having announced the Kingdom present in mystery form, the interim when the Church comes into its own, Jesus goes on to a new epoch of teaching. His coming death and resurrection are now openly revealed. The key phrase in Matthew 16:21 is: "From that time Jesus began to show his disciples . . ." (*see* Mark 8:31, 32; Luke 9:22). This new epoch of teaching continued until the end, as all three Synoptic Gospels make clear. The Great Transition is being made; there is to be a new period of redemptive history, a new body of God's people, a new message, and a new rule of life. Mosaic legalism shall be supplanted by a higher Kingdom Law, and that law shall in turn be qualified by a unique operation of God's grace in a redemptive, renewing ministry to the Church Age. No one can deny that in the Epistles this new message—so different in approach from that in the Synoptic Gospels—takes a central place. The Kingdom theme goes through a striking metamorphosis.

If, as the Epistles certify, the death and resurrection of Christ are so absolutely essential to the New Covenant, why then was so little even intimated about these matters before? If, indeed, as some suppose, the Kingdom is to be equated with the Church, why do we not find fundamental truths essential to the Church intermingled with earlier Kingdom teachings? If the Kingdom and the Church are virtually identical, why the virtual silence in John's Gospel, where theologically advanced truth for the Church is found? Why are these two areas of truth so ingeniously separated in Jesus' teaching, if we are to take the difference between the Synoptics and John seriously? Why is the Kingdom the single message before the national rejection, whereas the Church is the new message after that official rejection? Logical consistency demands our making a distinction fully appropriate to these facts.

Jesus reassured the disciples that His impending death would

not mean an abandonment of the Kingdom. Rather, its establishment would be consummated with His Second Coming. "For
the Son of man is to come with his angels in the glory of his
Father . . ." (Matthew 16:27). This is the first explicit reference in the Gospel narrative to the Second Advent, and quite
strikingly it comes immediately after Israel's rejection and the
announcement of the formation of the Church. To further reas-
sure the disciples at that time, Jesus was transfigured before the
eyes of the favored three—a prevision, no less, of ". . . the
Son of man coming in his kingdom" (Matthew 16:28). *All this
condensed in one continuous passage!* Just as strikingly, John,
who was one of the privileged three to be present on that occasion, did not write about it. It is our considered opinion that the
reason was consistent with John's purpose—he was not writing
about the glory of the King, but rather about the God who came
to save men from their sins in His own blood. And the presence
of Moses and Elijah on the Mount of Transfiguration suggests
that Jesus fulfilled the *law* (Moses) and was greeted by His precursor (Elijah). They both disappeared leaving "Jesus only" in
their midst, again suggesting His singular glory as King when
both of them have played their part and left the stage of divine
history.

Another promise which can only be viewed with the same lit-
eralness as other Kingdom concepts, is sounded by Jesus and
recorded by both Matthew and Luke: "Truly, I say to you, in
the new world, when the Son of man shall sit on his glorious
throne, you who have followed me will also sit on twelve
thrones, judging the twelve tribes of Israel" (Matthew 19:28; *see
also* Luke 22:28–30).

To correct a possible misunderstanding that the Kingdom was
to come in the immediate future, Jesus outlined in parabolic
form the rejection leading to the postponement of the Kingdom,
the ensuing interval in its unique characteristics, and the
Kingdom's certain future establishment. Of utmost importance

in this connection is the parable of the Pounds. This parable is recorded in Luke 19:11-27, and has no parallel in Matthew, indicating again that the Kingdom message is to be understood most fully when all three Synoptic Gospels are studied as a single body of truth.

The occasion and purpose of the parable are indicated in verse 11: ". . . because he was near to Jerusalem, and because they supposed that the kingdom of God was to appear immediately." It was on the following day that Jesus was to ride into Jerusalem, presenting Himself as the Messianic King, fulfilling every detail in accordance with Old Testament prophecy. The manner of this Kingdom offer to Israel, and the miracles which accompanied it, would naturally incline the disciples to suppose that the Kingdom was to be established at once, despite the crisis of official rejection which they had experienced just so recently. What an accurate forecast the parable afforded them!

Now what does this parable teach? During the nobleman's absence in a far country to receive for himself a kingdom and to return, the citizens repudiate him, saying, "We do not want this man to reign over us." In due time the nobleman returns, bringing his newly acquired kingly power with him. Immediately he executes judgment upon those who had repudiated him.

Several implications stand out. Israel hated and repudiated her Messiah-King. He returned to heaven and was there invested with His kingly right to reign. The nation Israel, represented by those citizens in the parable who repudiated the nobleman but remained until his return, shall officially maintain its national existence until He returns. Their enmity also remains! As to its length of time, the interim of His absence is kept indefinite, so the citizens maintain a vigilance, expecting His return. Similarly, the interim of our Lord's absence is kept indefinite as to its length of time. But His return is certain, His judgment upon those who repudiated Him is also certain, and He shall establish His Kingdom just as He said He would, and

prominently with those in that Kingdom whom He had first
known and who remained to receive Him. Israel at last has national existence.

Jesus' official entrance into Jerusalem, the governmental and
religious capital of Israel, was to present Himself as King. He
knew what faced Him there, for just prior to His entry, we hear
His sad lament and note its peculiar significance, "Would that
even today you knew the things that make for peace! But now
they are hid from your eyes." Pronouncing judgment upon
them, He continues, ". . . because you did not know the time
of your visitation" (*see* Luke 19:42, 44).

Matthew tells us that the very detail of His entry was in order
that Zechariah's prediction might be fulfilled (Matthew 21:4, 5;
see also Zechariah 9:9). Notably, Matthew restricts his quota-
tion of Zechariah to only the first part. Zechariah 9:10 goes on to
tell what the King will do when His reign is established. But
Matthew knew that the King had arrived, but had not occupied
His Messianic throne. So Matthew stops before he comes to that
part of Zechariah's prophecy, showing that Matthew did not believe that the Kingdom had arrived as it shall when Jesus returns
to establish it. There continues to be tension between that eschatological establishment of the Kingdom, and manifestation of
the Kingdom presently in real but highly restricted terms.

Continuing our sequence of events, note how differently Jesus
governs the public nature of these events, in contrast with
former occasions when He had strictly enjoined silence upon
His disciples with reference to any public acclamation of His
kingly claims (Matthew 16:20; Luke 9:21). Now there is no re-
buke from the lips of Jesus; the time for personal disclosure and
His official offer of Himself as King is at hand. The time for
national decision at the very governmental and religious heart of
the nation is at hand. This is the day that shall decide whether
Jerusalem shall become the blessed center of all nations, the
spiritual capital of the Kingdom of God on earth, or the terrible
monument of God's retributive justice.

Once again, according to the chronology of events in Matthew's account, Jesus turns to parables. This time it is a new series of Kingdom parables which present a composite picture of the Kingdom as something definitely future, definitely associated with the glorious advent of the King with great power and glory. Its establishment will be sudden, accompanied by a Messianic judgment of the wicked, and reward for the faithful. It is a picture of judgment on earth, judgment of living nations. Notably, it is a judgment inaugurated at the beginning of the Millennial Kingdom, not at its close. (Compare Matthew 25:31–46 with Revelation 20:1–15.)

Jesus' denunciation of the leaders of the nation is most fully recorded in Matthew 23:1–36. At the heart of His denunciation are the words: ". . . because you shut the kingdom of heaven against men; for you neither enter yourselves, nor allow those who would enter to go in" (v. 13). The representatives of the nation shut out Israel of that generation and many generations to come from their promised Kingdom. Jesus added, "Truly I say to you, all this will come upon this generation" (v. 36). It was nearly forty years before that judgment actually fell, the period when the Church was being formed—the period covered by the Book of Acts.

The King's final lament over Jerusalem, recorded in Matthew 23:37–39, has a significant focal point in verse 38: "Behold, your house is forsaken and desolate." Evidently this has primary reference to the Temple, for Matthew 24:1 continues, "Jesus left the temple . . . ." But His judgment is far more inclusive, incorporating both city and nation. No longer is it "my house" but "your house" (*see* Matthew 21:13). Still, the door of hope is left open with an implied promise: "I tell you, you will not see me again, until you say, 'Blessed is he who comes in the name of the Lord'" (Matthew 23:39). Isaiah saw the ultimate restoration of the nation, and wrote, "You shall no more be termed Forsaken, and your land shall no more be termed Desolate . . ." (Isaiah 62:4).

Now, in our Lord's last and longest eschatological discourse, He unfolds more fully the prophetic program of the end-time, giving special attention to the interim period (*see* Matthew 24, 25; Mark 13; Luke 21). Again, our Lord refers to a particular generation—not the generation then under judgment, but a future generation. The events of the end-time shall be accomplished in the space of a single generation. "Truly, I say to you, this generation will not pass away before all these things take place" (Mark 13:30). What generation? As in verse 29: "When you see these things taking place" (verses 5–28 record the sequence of *these things*). Thus, expectedly, all three Synoptic Gospels unite their testimony regarding the glorious advent of Christ as climaxing the end-time. Truly, the Kingdom in all its prophetic fulfillment is the burden of the Synoptic Gospels!

Just as significantly, this is not the burden of John's Gospel or the New Testament Epistles written to the churches. It does not become the central theme again until the final book of the New Testament, the only apocalyptic book of the New Testament. In his Gospel, John gives attention instead to the last hours of Jesus' ministry spent in intimate instruction of His disciples who shall carry on after His death, resurrection and ascension. The theme does not concern the Kingdom, but the interim. It would seem that this intimate instruction would surely be concerned with the Kingdom as it is manifested in the Church, but such is not the case. This aspect of Kingdom truth does not seem to be dominant at all. Yet this "theological gospel" in every other way shows its great comprehensiveness of truths which the Church needs for the interim. The Upper Room Discourse occupies all of four chapters in John (13 through 16). Strikingly, whereas the Kingdom had been mentioned at least five times during the Last Supper, in this discourse, which immediately follows, there is no mention of it at all! Jesus is not preparing the disciples for some partial fulfillment of the Kingdom; this seems a somewhat incidental reality. He is more concerned to prepare them for the interim when the fullness of the eschatological Kingdom is delayed and the King absent. Jesus speaks of His own spiritual presence and ministry, but not in Kingdom terms. He emphasizes His physical return for His own, and the coming and ministry of the Holy Spirit in His absence. The Synoptic Gospels nowhere teach the present ministry of the Holy Spirit to believers, content only to include John the Baptist's single allusion to the coming baptizing work of the Holy Spirit, and the sin against the Holy Spirit. He makes it plain that the Holy Spirit will not come until He, Jesus, ascends to the Father. But so far as the Holy Spirit's work in the lives of believers is concerned, this is left to John's Gospel and to the Epistles. Once more, the separation of truth having to do with the Kingdom directly, and truth having to do with the believers making up the Church, is apparent. In John's record of the wonderful prayer of Jesus, which follows immediately upon the Upper Room Discourse, the emphasis is upon the need for the disciples to be kept from the evil one (John 17:15). That prayer envisions the disciples living and working in the kingdom of Satan; Kingdom conditions are not developing, only suffering and persecution lie ahead. The message of John does not supplement that of the Synoptic Gospels; it is to a large extent an altogether different message!

When Jesus was present as the Messianic King in their midst, the disciples "tasted of the powers of the age to come" (*see* Hebrews 6:5). He refers to this in a remarkable passage found only in Luke. It is in the context of His preparing the disciples for the changed conditions they shall encounter during the interim. "[Jesus says] 'When I sent you out with no purse or bag or sandals, did you lack anything?' They said, 'Nothing.' He said to them, 'But now, let him who has a purse take it, and likewise a bag. And let him who has no sword sell his mantle and buy one' " (Luke 22:35, 36). How incompatible this sounds in relation to Jesus' Kingdom teachings and the Kingdom Law! It should be obvious that the same social conditions do not pre-

vail in the New Aeon of the consummated Kingdom, and the
Old Aeon in which the Church of the interim finds itself. The
necessity of adapting Kingdom Law to the interim seems a logical deduction. It is this deduction that shall be seen to affect our
understanding of Jesus' teaching on divorce and remarriage in
the Synoptic Gospels.

We have seen how Jesus was at first sent only to "the lost
sheep of the house of Israel" (*see* Matthew 10:6). This enables
us to understand John's terse summary word at the opening of
his Gospel: "He came to his own house, and his own people
received him not" (John 1:11). The reference is to His national
home. As the covenant of God with the Jews was a national one,
so also must be Christ's acceptance or rejection. From the beginning of God's covenants with Israel, their blessings were national blessings, and their punishments national punishments.
Furthermore, whatever was decided by the appointed heads of
the nation was regarded as the act and will of the nation.

Now, the nation Israel must be purged by judgment in preparation for the Kingdom. As John the Baptist came to a nation
no longer worthy of its covenant relationship with God, and
preached repentance, so it may be expected that any re-offer of
the Kingdom to Israel following their rejection of the Messiah
would also stress the preparatory aspect of repentance. In our
study of the Book of Acts we shall see this to be so; it explains
the emphasis upon repentance in Acts.

When Israel refused her King, Jesus quoted a passage from
Psalms 118:22, 23 to show that such rejection had been prophet-
ically anticipated (*see* Matthew 21:42). Then He declared,
"Therefore I tell you, the kingdom of God will be taken from
you and given to a nation producing the fruits of it" (Matthew
21:43). This follows by a few chapters the announcement of the
founding of the Church. In harmony with the mystery parables
of Matthew 13 which declare the hidden form of the Kingdom in
its partial manifestation during this age, we can understand this

declaration to refer to the Church. Dispensationalists usually see this as a reference to a repentant, restored Israel in the consummation. Non-Dispensationalists usually see this as a reference to the Church. It seems too much to say that Jesus was uttering an irrevocable indictment against Israel as such, for this would run counter to all the covenants God had made with that nation, and with many Scriptures which we have noted in this study. But it seems natural to see a reference to the people of God who were formed to continue God's redemptive program after Israel had officially been rejected. Even the terminology would seem congruous inasmuch as we read in 1 Peter 2:9, 10 concerning the Church: "But you are a chosen race, a royal priesthood, a holy nation . . . that you may declare the wonderful deeds of him who called you out of darkness into his marvelous light. Once you were no people but now you are God's people; once you had not received mercy, but now you have received mercy." How the Church adapts to this partial manifestation of the Kingdom which is breaking through in advance of the eschatological Kingdom is certainly the burden, not of the Synoptic Gospels, but of the Epistles. This affects the ethical demands and their partial fulfillment; it especially affects our view of how failure is dealt with. It is here that the full unfolding of God's grace in the teaching of the Epistles becomes our ultimate guide.

In summary, when the nation Israel rejected the Kingdom offer, those individuals who had accepted it were constituted the new people of God, the true sons of the Kingdom, the incipient Church of the interim. The Church's mission is, in part, to witness to the Kingdom in its present hidden form and in its coming consummation. But it should be kept clear that while the Church includes the people of the Kingdom, it is not itself the Kingdom. The visible Church can never be, nor can it produce, the Kingdom of God. This is an eschatological event which is God's inbreaking. The many sayings about entering the Kingdom are not

equivalent to entering the Church. In the early preaching in
Acts, it is impossible to substitute the word *church* for the word
kingdom. But in all of this, there is no reason why God's Kingdom, God's rule, cannot manifest itself in two different ways at
two different times, accomplishing the same ultimate redemptive
end. Jesus simply introduced a previously unforeseen era of the
Kingdom of God, an era that is limited to a partial fulfillment. As
the consummation awaits the age to come when there shall be a
new order, so the righteousness of the Kingdom can be
genuinely experienced in this present age, but the perfect righteousness of the Kingdom, like the Kingdom itself, awaits the eschatological consummation. The righteousness of the Kingdom
is attainable in part, if not in perfection, and thus the Kingdom
ethical demands are absolute and uncompromised. But the question remains—what is the practical reality in the interim? What
is to be expected during the time between the times, when the
imperfect, partial fulfillment necessarily incorporates failures?
Do the Epistles go beyond the Synoptic Gospels in the ethical
development of grace and realized forgiveness? What was the
direction the Church would take? How do the Epistles conceive
the real life of the Church in the interim? And most explicitly,
how are the issues of divorce and remarriage managed under
these conditions?

As the Kingdom was present in dynamic power in the earthly
Person and ministry of Jesus, it is present now in His spiritual
presence and power. But as He is not present in fullness, neither
are the powers of the Kingdom present in fullness. The Kingdom
Law cannot be perfectly realized. When Jesus comes again, His
presence, word, and power will have a new and effectual reality
which cannot be realized now. So we are to see that fulfillment
of the Kingdom ethic is potentially possible, and in given instances is, in fact, highly fulfilled in the present. But the element
of failure, like the need for progressive sanctification of each
believer, is a fact of this age. The tension between the partial
fulfillment in present history, and the eschatological consumma-

tion, is reflected in the ethical tension between the Kingdom ethic declared in its absolute form, and the necessity for a unique ministry of renewing grace during the Church's existence in the Old Aeon.

Before moving on to the specific question of how the Kingdom ethic is to be adapted to the Church Age, we turn to another question that shall be the subject of the next chapter. Inevitably, some will ask, "But at the beginning of the Church age, wasn't the message concerned with the Kingdom? Isn't this what we find in the Book of Acts? The preaching of the Kingdom evidently didn't stop after Jesus was crucified; is it not possible that the Kingdom is now spiritualized, and thus to be literally and perfectly fulfilled now? Would we not then have to say that the Kingdom Law, like the Kingdom itself, is in full effect—as much as it ever shall be? Would not the divorce-and-marriage sayings of Jesus then be the new law to be held in full force?"

This interpretation of the Kingdom as equated with the Church is still so pervasive in Christendom that it deserves at least a short chapter in our study. For half a century American Protestantism was subject to a liberal theology which equated Church and Kingdom. Notably, liberal Protestantism majored in the Synoptic Gospels in its preaching and teaching, all but neglecting the doctrinal books of the New Testament: the Epistles. An idealistic Kingdom ethic was preached; the Synoptic Gospels established the parameters. Liberal Protestantism was "building the Kingdom." Inevitably a reaction formed; the ethic was said by many to be "the impossible possibility" in itself. It was seen to be a radicalized ethic, an absolute ethic uncompromised by man's inability. But it drove many an erstwhile liberal scholar to pay attention once more to the eschatological aspects of the Kingdom which Jesus preached. The end-time Kingdom and the present manifestation are different in many respects, and so is present adaptation of eschatological ethics.

Before taking this up in detail, the following chapter will consider the true import of the Kingdom as it was preached in the early days of the Church and chronicled in the Book of Acts. We will seek to show that the present preform of the Kingdom is different from the eschatological Kingdom in Acts, and hence the ethical demands of the eschatological Kingdom may very well stand in need of special adaptation to the preform of the Kingdom as manifested in the Church during the interim and under the conditions of the Old Aeon in which it has its existence.

4

Seeing the Book of Acts Aright

On the cross Jesus prayed, "Father, forgive them; for they know not what they do" (Luke 23:34). How do we interpret this prayer? Was Jesus truly asking for a genuine forgiveness from the Father for those who were putting Him to death? Is such forgiveness available in answer to the prayer of the Son of God? And whom did Jesus have in mind? Only the Roman soldiers who executed the sentence? Or all Israel that had rejected Him and was responsible nationally for the accusation which sent Him to the cross? One can only conjecture, in the absence of biblical commentary, but it is at least intriguing to think that the Kingdom was re-offered to Israel in the period of time which followed His ascension and the execution of temporal judgment upon the nation nearly forty years later. Judgment demonstrably was delayed, and it is this period of time that is covered by the Book of Acts. The God who so often extends a second chance to those who turn from Him, re-offers the Kingdom to the very generation responsible for Israel's rejection of Christ and their own condemnation.

Why did God not execute judgment immediately upon Israel following the crucifixion of their King? Can we not believe that God in His sovereign providence had some important purpose in view? The Book of Acts supplies the answer to these questions. It is more than a transitional period during which the Church is established for this age. The nation Israel is once again called to repentance. And because the first half of Acts is concerned with

a message to the Jews, we can expect to find both the Kingdom
and the Church present in this transitional book. For the Church
now exists historically, Acts being the Book which records its
establishment with the coming of the Holy Spirit to form the
Body of Christ at Pentecost. The Kingdom, while not present,
occupies a large place in apostolic preaching as an imminent
possibility. And because of the unique circumstances of this
period, the imminent possibility of the Kingdom's establishment
was present. The very same generation of Israel which had rejected and crucified the Messiah was now, following His resurrection and ascension, being called to repentance and acceptance of Him. The witness to His resurrection by apostles empowered by the Holy Spirit makes for a new appeal to this generation of Jews. Will the nation repent of its sin against Jesus,
and recognize Him as their Messiah?

Israel was not yet abandoned as the people with whom the
covenants had been made, nor had this generation had its final
opportunity. The apostles are not told to turn immediately and
completely to the Gentiles. On the contrary, it is explicitly
stated that while the disciples were to make disciples of all nations (Matthew 28:19), they were to follow a definite order of
procedure: first Jerusalem, Israel's capital city; then Judea; followed by Samaria; and then on to the end of the earth (Acts
1:8). Whereas formerly the witness was restricted to Israel alone
(Matthew 10:5, 6), now it is to be carried to all the earth. However, the order of procedure indicates that Israel's priority still
holds. And since there is nothing to suggest that God had yet
judged the nation and turned from it, or that only individual
Jews were to be witnessed to, it must be supposed that God is
once again in His mercy giving Israel another chance to repent
and prepare for the Kingdom to come. *In such an event, the
Kingdom might be imminent!* It is our task to see if this is not
the case as we look at the Book of Acts, keeping in mind the
continuity of the Kingdom offer.

F. F. Bruce orients us with his comment: "The *Acts of the Apostles* is the name given since about the middle of the second century A.D. to the second volume of a *History of Christian Origins* composed by a first-century Christian and dedicated to a certain Theophilus. The first volume of this *History* is also extant as one of the twenty-seven documents included in the New Testament canon; it is the work ordinarily known as *The Gospel according to St. Luke.*" Bruce adds, "The primary purpose of *Acts* cannot be considered in isolation from the purpose of the 'former treatise' of which it is the continuation." For this reason, Bruce calls the Gospel and Acts "Part I and Part II." There seems no doubt at the very outset that the Book of Acts continues to outline the transition from the message of the Kingdom directed to Israel to the universal message directed in quite different terms to Jews and Gentiles alike. The Kingdom is to be understood in the same way as in the Synoptic Gospels.

In the first chapter, the disciples ask Jesus, "Lord, will you at this time restore the kingdom to Israel? (Acts 1:6). Now, if the Church were to be equated with the Kingdom as some suppose, would not Jesus have taken this opportunity to instruct the disciples that the Kingdom was no longer related in any way nationally to Israel? Would He not have begun immediately to help them adjust their thinking to the new reality? Surely He would have disenchanted them of such nationalistic hopes if they were no longer appropriate! But this He did not do. Jesus simply replied that they were not given to know the time of the Kingdom's appearance. The disciples had made the right assumption—and this in spite of the teaching of Matthew 13 and the parables of the Kingdom in mystery form—that the Kingdom was primarily eschatological and to come at a future time. They knew that the Kingdom was not established on earth. Jesus implicitly confirms this. He also tacitly confirms their expectation that the Kingdom shall be the same as the prophets had foretold, not a different Kingdom. And although Jesus had earlier announced that it had been taken away from that generation, there is no question on the part of the disciples that the Kingdom had been forever removed from Israel, but only that it would involve a future generation of God's covenant people.

Peter, in his great Pentecostal address in Acts 2, refers to the prophecy of Joel 2:28–32, saying that the miraculous testimony of Pentecost was something to be expected prior to the establishment of the Messianic Kingdom. He then answers the question of how a crucified man could possibly be the Messianic King. He cites Psalms 16:8–11 to show that Jesus had proved His right to the Davidic throne by rising from the dead (Acts 2:24–32). Peter then refers to Psalm 110 to prove that David himself had envisioned Messiah as first ascending into heaven for a session at God's right hand until His foes were brought into subjection by the coming of His Kingdom (vv. 33–35). Peter ends by saying that Jesus had been made both "Lord and Christ" (v. 36). *Kurios* is the Greek title which the Jews themselves used to translate the sacred name of Jehovah in the Hebrew, while *Christos* is the Greek equivalent of the Hebrew Messiah, the Anointed King.

Now, if Jesus were the Messianic King, as Peter had just proved, and if remission of sins could extend even to the same generation of Jews who had taken responsibility for Christ's death, then the conclusion was that the restoration of the long-awaited Kingdom to Israel under Messiah was still a possibility to that same generation. The apostolic signs and wonders confirmed this possibility in their minds, for these were signs of the Kingdom predicted by the prophets. And these were the very same signs which marked the coming Kingdom as offered by the Messiah before His death.

There is no mention of the Church in chapter 2 of Acts, suggesting that it did not yet occupy the center of the stage in God's redemptive history, as it came to do later when the apostolic offer of the King had met with official rejection once more.

Surely, if there had been no re-offer of the Kingdom to Israel during the period of the Acts, we might have expected a rather full disclosure of the nature of the Church early in that period. The fact that such a disclosure was delayed demands some explanation. The true explanation must be found in the transitional character of the period covered by Acts. Because the re-offer was made, the period begins with the Kingdom in the foreground, the Church in the background. To the still-continuing nation Israel, the Kingdom offer is being made once more; to the newly formed Church, both Jew and Gentile are being directed as believers. These two movements coexist side by side in the ministry of the apostles. Notably, Peter is the designated Apostle to the Jews, even as Paul later on is designated Apostle to the Gentiles. That this has vital significance at this period is clear when seen in contrast with Paul's later declaration to the Galatians, "There is neither Jew nor Greek . . ." (Galatians 3:28). It was at the end of this period that Paul, imprisoned in Rome, announces that he is turning to the Gentiles because of Israel's impenitence. Contemporaneously, he writes his prison Epistles which contain a disclosure of the uniqueness of the Church. Thus, the Book of Acts, while a genuine segment of Church history, is more than that; it records the parallel ministry to Israel and to the Church for a short period before temporal judgment fell upon Israel to end its existence as a nation for that time.

Returning to the sequence of events and teaching in Acts, we note that shortly after Pentecost a remarkable miracle at the Temple gate was acknowledged by the chief priests and elders (Acts 4:16). Peter once again gives an address, directing it to the nation: "Men of Israel . . ." (Acts 3:12). Looking back upon the condemning act of that generation in crucifying their Messiah, Peter now declares:

> . . . I know that you acted in ignorance, as did also your rulers. But what God foretold by the mouth of all the prophets, that his Christ should suffer, he thus fulfilled. Repent, therefore, and turn

again, that your sins may be blotted out, that times of refreshing
may come from the presence of the Lord, and that he may send
the Christ appointed for you, Jesus, whom heaven must receive
until the time for establishing all that God spoke by the mouth of
his holy prophets from of old . . . . You are the sons . . . of
the covenant which God gave to your fathers . . . . God, having
raised up his servant, sent him to you first, to bless you in turning
every one of you from your wickedness.

Acts 3:17–21, 25, 26

Israel's "ignorance" justifies another offer of the King and
Kingdom from a gracious God.

Peter, you note, is careful to identify Jesus with the great
kingly servant of Isaiah 40 through 53. And now, if Israel will
meet these spiritual conditions, not only will its sins be blotted
out, but especially important, God will send Jesus back! Once
again, God is offering King and Kingdom together to that generation of Israel. As the original offer of the Kingdom was made
first to Israel during the days of His flesh, so now, having been
raised from the dead and seated at the right hand of the Father
in heaven, the offer is once more made to Israel first. Peter was
appointed the great leader of this offer, and nothing could be
clearer than that Peter was prepared for this ministry to Israel in
a way that Paul, who dominated the scene later on, was not. It is
a mistake to suppose that Peter was an apostle to individual
Jews only, or to the Jewish community as culturally distinct
from the Gentiles to whom Paul was sent. This isn't the point at
all. Peter spoke to the nation Israel as such. There was a fundamental need for unrepentant Israel to restore its place as God's
covenant people, if the God of Abraham was once again to draw
near to them. So long as the nation continued to exist, God gave
them further opportunity to turn to Him.

This re-offer of the Kingdom to Israel was intimated in Jesus'
parable recorded in Matthew 22:1–10. A certain king gave a
marriage feast for his son. Those invited would not come, some
even mistreating the servants sent with the invitation. The king

sent a second invitation to those who had refused the first. When this was rejected, the king sent his troops to destroy the people and burn their city. He then sent his servants with the invitation to any and all whom they could find. The application is rather obvious to any student who can look back upon the redemptive history of that time. The invitation was first sent out to a special people whom the king had reason to invite. He sent the invitation again when it was first refused. This most certainly is a reference to the coming of the King, Israel's Messiah, and his invitation to Israel to the wedding feast of His Son. When Israel refused, a second offer was made. But this only led to persecution and death for the servants sent with the invitation. True to His prediction, the servants of God were murdered and persecuted in the period of the Acts such as had not occurred during the days of His flesh. But judgment followed, even as it fell upon Jerusalem in A.D. 70. Our interpretation of the Book of Acts fits precisely with the major events depicted in this predictive parable.

As there were thirty-two miracles to authenticate the first offer of the Kingdom, so in Acts there are thirty miracles recorded for the same purpose—a striking similarity. How unique was this period of nearly forty years between Pentecost and the destruction of Jerusalem! By contrast, how silent is the period following the destruction of Jerusalem with reference to public miracles and the preaching of the Kingdom. The nation has been dispersed and national unity destroyed, so that national response could no longer be made to the invitation of God.

The great public miracles which occurred during the period covered by the Book of Acts evidently are powers which really belong to the Millennial Kingdom yet to come. Their appearance was to authenticate the offer then being made to Israel. Unquestionably, this is the meaning of the reference in Hebrews 6:5: "[Who] have tasted . . . the powers of the age to come." The relative absence of such miracles in the Church Age from that period on can be understood with this in mind. This does not indicate that the miracle-working power of God ceased altogether, but the relative prominence of such publicly authenticating signs did indeed cease.

The first seven chapters of Acts show the response of the Jews to be a progressive hardening and opposition. The first movement of this culminates in the death of Stephen (chap. 7). The second development covers an almost equal number of chapters, culminating in Paul's address at Antioch (chap. 13). The third development of Israel's opposition culminates in Paul's imprisonment and his subsequent conference with the Jewish leaders in Rome (chap. 28). Let us review these developments in a bit more detail.

The record of official hardening and persecution begins in Acts 4:1–3, directly following Peter's offer of the Kingdom on the condition of repentance. It reached its crisis when Stephen was stoned to death for accusing the Jewish authorities of resisting the Holy Spirit, killing the prophets, and murdering their Messiah who had come (Acts 7:51–60). Strikingly, Paul (then Saul) was among those who inaugurated the great Jewish persecution of Christians at that time. In this connection, what an additional authentication to Israel it was that this chief persecutor became a Christian and a leading Apostle (Acts 9:1–31)! God was even choosing authenticating signs from within the very leadership of the unrepentant nation. But at this part of Luke's record in Acts, it is the intransigence of Israel that is most prominent. This is the entire burden of Stephen's long address which occupies nearly all of chapter 7.

In the Great Transition recorded in Acts, there is an evident alternation of the message to Israel and the message to the Gentiles who were now being brought into the newly formed Church. Chapter 10 inserts the record of the conversion of Cornelius, a Gentile, and the revelation that Gentiles were not excluded from God's salvation. But the climax of the Great Transition is reached in chapter 13 with the long address of Paul in the synagogue at Antioch. Like Peter before him, Paul recounts the preparation of Israel for the coming of Christ, reiterating the theme of His coming to Israel: ". . . to us has been sent the message of this salvation" (v. 26), *us* referring to Israel. But Paul is not at all concerned to offer the Kingdom to Israel. Their opposition was by this point already determined, and further- more, this was not Paul's commission. On the succeeding Sab- bath, Paul unambiguously declared, ". . . It was necessary that the word of God should be spoken first to you. Since you thrust it from you, and judge yourselves to be unworthy of eternal life, behold we turn to the Gentiles" (v. 46).

From this time on it is a record of massive opposition and deepening intolerance to the message by Israel. Notably, the Great Transition was not abrupt. In chapter 18 Paul is still preaching to the Jews that the Christ was Jesus. When, how- ever, the message was further rejected, he said, " . . Your blood be upon your heads! I am innocent. From now on I will go to the Gentiles" (v. 6). The transition was nearly effected.

Now follows Paul's visit to Israel's capital city, Jerusalem. Here begins the condemnation of Paul that led to his appeal for trial before Caesar, his removal to Rome, and imprisonment there. From reading the last fifteen verses which close the book, one gains an impressive confirmation that Acts is the Book of the Great Transition—transition to the Gentiles with the univer- sal message of salvation to all mankind. It is the transition of finally turning away from Israel, with the primary message of the Kingdom now postponed in favor of developing the concept of the interim Church. This is brought to its culmination in this final section, where Paul gathers the local leaders of the Jews and indicates to them that the reason he is imprisoned is "be- cause of the hope of Israel" (*see* 28:20). Then we read in verse 23: ". . . And he expounded the matter to them from morning till evening, testifying to the kingdom of God and trying to convince them about Jesus both from the law of Moses and from the prophets." Receiving a mixed response, Paul concludes with a final judgment, quoting Isaiah 6:9, 10, which predicted Israel's intransigence. His last word is: "Let it be known to you then that this salvation of God has been sent to the Gentiles; they will listen" (v. 28).

Notice carefully, Paul does not say that the message of the Kingdom has been sent to the Gentiles, but "this salvation." Words are carefully chosen. The comment closing the Book of Acts is to the effect that Paul welcomed those who visited him in his imprisonment, "preaching the kingdom of God and teaching about the Lord Jesus Christ (vv. 30, 31). The dual emphasis he continued to his last days. The Book of Acts begins in Jerusalem and ends in Rome—how truly prophetic of the whole course of things! The Great Transition has taken place, and from now on the preaching of the Kingdom is that of a future reign when Jesus returns, and of the shadow of that Kingdom, as Christians are waiting sons of a Kingdom to come, yet presently subject to the rule of the King and thus manifesting the Kingdom in a hidden form. That they shall not perfectly fulfill the law of the Kingdom is made clear elsewhere in the Epistles. That grace shall meet them at the point of failure, and that realized forgiveness and redemptive renewal has supplanted legalistic penalties, is also revealed elsewhere. But the way of God's unchanging righteousness is before them in the law of the Kingdom, and the power of the Holy Spirit is made available to them to fulfill that righteousness to the extent that they appropriate that power. So here is the book that begins with Peter, Apostle to the Jews, and closes with Paul, Apostle to the Gentiles. It is the book that begins in Jerusalem and ends in Rome, the book that deals faithfully with the re-offer of the Kingdom to the nation Israel before judgment descends, and closes by turning from Israel to the whole world. The Kingdom message shall become once again an eschatological hope for the most part; the Church shall take center stage as God's new thing among men. As the Book of Acts together with the Synoptic Gospels faithfully portrayed the offer of the Kingdom to the people whom God had covenanted to receive it, now the Epistles together with John's Gospel shall faithfully convey the message of the New Covenant.

The Book of Acts seems to conclude abruptly, as though unfinished. Many have surmised that a sequel was planned but never written. But the Book of Acts has completed its message—the Great Transition has been made. As the Kingdom offer is once again abruptly rejected by the Jews, so the Book of Acts ends abruptly. Only judgment awaits Israel—destruction of the capital city including the Temple. The people shall shortly be dispersed over the face of the earth and the land taken away for many centuries to come. The nation would be restored at a later time in history and once again prepared to participate nationally in the Kingdom when it is consummated with the coming of the King. But for now the covenanted Kingdom is no longer an imminent possibility for Israel.

So we leave the Book of Acts to enter the Church Age, an age which is governed by the Epistles essentially, as those letters were written for that explicit purpose. The Epistles are truly theological, with very little intermingling of history. John's Gospel is unique in that it combines the historical with the theological in a way not characteristic of the Synoptic Gospels. This, of course, is not to say that the Synoptic Gospels do not contain teaching directly applicable to the Church. But great care must be exercised when making these applications from the Synoptics, inasmuch as Jesus is sometimes speaking within the context of the Mosaic Law and at other times is addressing conditions which will prevail only in the eschatological Kingdom. There are at times dual applications—Kingdom Law which has a distinctly legal cast appropriate to the social order of the realized Kingdom, which nonetheless makes a direct demand upon God's people now. The problem is in deciding when the legalistic features are applicable and when not. When is the absolute demand qualified by the conditions of the Old Aeon under which the Church has its life, and how is the conditional will of God exercised in the redemptive ways of grace? This question has significant bearing on the matter of divorce and remarriage.

The message of the Kingdom, for all practical purposes, is heard no more. The period covered by Acts began with the Kingdom as its major emphasis, the Church at first having almost no distinguishably separate identity—although by now it is well established. As the period progresses, the Church begins to assume a more prominent place, while the possibility of the Kingdom being established becomes more remote to the central emphasis of the apostolic message. Not once in Acts is it ever suggested that the Kingdom is now to be conceptualized primarily or only as a spiritualized Kingdom. This is as foreign to the Book of Acts as it is to the Synoptic Gospels. The consummation of the Kingdom still lies in the future.

Acts 14:22: ". . . that through many tribulations we must enter the kingdom of God," refers to the future eschatological Kingdom and to the practical problem of how to face opposition, the response of faith being an evidence that they are sons of that coming Kingdom. Entry into the Kingdom is through the New Birth. The meaning here can only be that their future entrance into the eschatological Kingdom shall be through present tribulation. But this is not to be counted an evil, much less an evidence of God's lack of care. This is simply the reality of the confrontation between light and darkness in this world. As the children of God through Jesus Christ, Christians are at the same time sons of that coming Kingdom. But since that Kingdom is theirs by anticipation, they are to witness throughout their days of tribulation to the powers of the age to come that have already manifested themselves in their lives; this is the reality of the Kingdom in its present form.

When we survey the twenty-one Epistles of the New Testament, each of them sent to the Church—in most instances to individual churches, then on to others in a circular coverage—it is striking that no Epistle is addressed: "To the saints in the Kingdom of heaven." We are no longer moving in the sphere of truth dominated by this terminology of the Kingdom. In fact, terminology becomes highly decisive at this juncture of our understanding. For example, the word *church* is found only three times in the Synoptic Gospels—all three, in fact, in one brief section of one of the Gospels (*see* Matthew 16:18; 18:17). The word *kingdom,* on the other hand, which dominates the Synoptic Gospels, is found with frequency in Acts, as is also the word *church,* which occurs some nineteen times. But in the Epistles, the word *church* is found no less than sixty-seven times, whereas the word *kingdom* is found only eighteen times—on the average less than once per New Testament Epistle. To suggest that this is because of the non-Jewish milieu is unsatisfactory, and only further reduces the possibility that the Kingdom is to be understood by the early Church as prominently manifesting itself under a new form. There can be little question that the New Testament Epistles are mainly concerned with the Church in the interim, with her career and character prior to the coming of the King and the establishment of the Kingdom on earth. The very term *kingdom* is frequently used in the Epistles to refer to the divine rule. When it is a present reality, it may be *preached* (Acts 8:12; 19:8; 28:23, 31), *entered* (Colossians 1:13), or *manifested* (1 Corinthians 4:20); but nowhere do we read that it must be *received.* Nor is the Church ever spoken of as the ultimate end, but always as that which is oriented toward that ultimate end—the eschatological Kingdom yet to come. The present age can be seen as a time of preparation and anticipation, of tasting the powers of the age to come, and of orienting life toward the ethical absolutes which have been revealed for perfect fulfillment in the future.

We who are members of the Church in this age, also sons of

the coming Kingdom by anticipation, profit by knowing just what are the absolute demands of God's unchanging righteousness. We understand something of what righteousness in the Kingdom Age will incorporate, and how its social rule will differ from this age of the Church. In many ways we can determine what ethical objectives should impress themselves upon our own conduct. This, however, is a far cry from assuming that Kingdom Law can be perfectly realized in the present. Rather, it orients us just as realistically to this fallen aeon. It enables us to appropriate the conditions of grace which are set forth so fully in the Epistles. The principles of grace provide for our being and doing, lead us to the inward enabling power of the Holy Spirit, and show us God's gracious response to failure and sin. His response in grace is so different from the imposition of binding legal sanctions! The divorce-and-remarriage teachings of Jesus must be viewed from the perspective of these principles of grace, and not made a new law to the Church. The enormity of the consequences following on such a distinction cannot be overestimated!

5

Matthew's Special Contexts

We've remarked already that the words of Jesus on divorce and remarriage are found only in the Synoptic Gospels, not in John's Gospel at all. These words of His are nowhere repeated in the Epistles, although Paul alludes to them in his First Letter to the Corinthians. However, his teaching differs from that of Jesus, inasmuch as Paul allows an exception not mentioned by Jesus, while at the same time failing to take notice of the exception attributed to Jesus by Matthew. That these words of Jesus are confined to the Synoptics is a fact that should signal our close attention, especially since we have studied the unique Kingdom setting of the Gospels in previous chapters. While Jesus' words on divorce and remarriage are found in all three Synoptic Gospels, we shall be able to reduce our extended examination of the four separate texts down to the two in Matthew.

All three Synoptic Gospels represent the same tradition, that of Jesus' Kingdom teachings. To consider the most representative texts is, therefore, to include the others insofar as they can be assimilated into the same perspective. Two of the four statements attributed to Jesus are in Matthew. The contexts in Matthew represent a fully developed setting and so possibly the latest transmission. Luke is deficient of any context whatever, giving us an isolated statement. Mark's version is parallel in nearly every detail, and since it is generally conceded that Mark was written earlier and served as a source for Matthew (along with the possible Q source), Matthew represents the later, perhaps higher level of transmission.

Not only is the passage in Luke strangely isolated from any immediate context to which it can be related, but Luke was equally dependent upon the same sources as Matthew to a large degree. Mark is almost completely duplicated in Matthew and Luke. The best text of Mark contains some 661 verses, of which at least 610 are paralleled in either Matthew or Luke, and a large proportion in both. Only 3 of 88 paragraphs in Mark are absent in both the other Gospels. Mark seems unquestionably a source document for both Matthew and Luke. So, inasmuch as Luke has but a brief statement which has no other context than that of a Gospel in the Kingdom-teachings tradition, we need not consider it separately from Matthew. Apparently Luke found no other place for its inclusion, and simply inserted it where he did. The single question relating to Mark and Luke which must be considered later on is why neither of them contains the exceptive clause, "except on the ground of unchastity." This exceptive clause is found in both statements attributed to Jesus by Matthew. For the purpose of our examination of the texts in Matthew predominantly, suffice it to say here that any movement away from the orders of creation—which made no provision for divorce and remarriage—must be the subject of our major investigation, at any rate.

Matthew becomes for us a very special context apart from the other two Synoptic Gospels. Two of the four statements of Jesus are found here. The two statements which contain the exceptive clause are both found here. Both statements have significant contexts, one the Sermon on the Mount, the other the debate with the Pharisees. One context relates to the Kingdom, the other to the Mosaic economy. How either or both relate to the Christian economy under grace is our chief problem. And if any one of the Synoptic Gospels is more systematically demonstrative of every major consideration at the heart of the Kingdom, it is Matthew. If ever there is a need to look at New Testament teaching with an eye to its primary orientation to the theme of

Israel's Kingdom, it most certainly is the divorce-and-remarriage passages in the Synoptics, and especially in Matthew!

Matthew stands uniquely as the link between the Old and New Testaments, and is properly regarded as a transition book deserving its place at the beginning of the New Testament. It, like Mark and Luke but even more so, stands as it were with one foot in the old Mosaic administration, the other foot in the age of the New Covenant. Quite fittingly, Matthew was written to Jewish readers. Both the terminology and the concepts of Matthew were familiar to the people of Israel. For them Matthew especially breaks a silence of four hundred years, between the prophet Malachi whose message closed the Old Testament canon, and the birth of Jesus. Now to Matthew was granted the privilege of showing that Jesus was born to be the King of the Jews. More than any other of the Gospels, Matthew's is allied with the Hebrew Scriptures in theme and tone. Their subjects are its subjects: the Messiah, Israel, the law, the Kingdom, and prophecy. There are 129 Old Testament references in Matthew; 53 are citations, 76 allusions. These are taken from no less than 25 of the 39 Old Testament books, and represent each of the Old Testament major divisions—the Law, the Psalms, and the Prophets. Of the 129 references, 89 are made by our Lord Himself. Ten times Matthew uses the phrase *that it might be fulfilled*. There are more Old Testament quotations recorded in Matthew than in Mark, Luke, and John combined. Sixteen times one phrase runs through the Gospel: "All this was done that it might be fulfilled which was spoken by the prophet, saying . . . ." Matthew's one great overriding purpose is to present Jesus as Israel's King. Everything in his Gospel contributes toward this single end. While Mark and Luke are in this same essential tradition, they are both governed by this purpose to a much lesser degree.

Matthew's Gospel is built around (1) the proclamation of the

Kingdom, (2) the interpretation of the Kingdom, and (3) the administration of the Kingdom. His purpose is perceived in the opening verse, "The book of the genealogy of Jesus Christ, the son of David, the son of Abraham." This expression is found nowhere else in the New Testament. Jesus is shown to have the undisputed claim to Israel's throne. This title *Son of David* is applied to Christ ten times in Matthew, whereas *Son of Abraham* does not appear again. In 2 Samuel 7:4–17 we read of God's covenant with David for the King who shall sit upon David's throne forever. And interestingly, as if to make this emphasis all the stronger, of all the kings listed in the genealogy of Christ, only David is called *king,* and this occurs twice.

Matthew goes on to the birth of the King as it answers to Old Testament prophecy, also narrating the search of the wise men for the King—an incident found only in Matthew. Then follows the flight into Egypt, the birthplace of the nation Israel, and the attempt of Herod against the King's life. Soon thereafter we are introduced to the herald of the King, John the Baptist, and his message, "Repent, for the kingdom of heaven is at hand" (Matthew 3:2). The expression *the kingdom of the heavens* is a Semitic idiom which would be meaningless except to Jewish hearers, occurring alone in Matthew, and there some thirty-four times.

Early in Matthew the grand message of his Gospel is sounded. What a contrast with Paul's phrase in Acts 20:24: *the gospel of the grace of God.* These are two distinct messages and are never confused. There is perfect continuity between Matthew's message and Old Testament teaching. Matthew is the Gospel of the Kingdom. The gospel of the grace of God took on a whole new understanding after Calvary and the resurrection.

Appropriately, Matthew tells of the anointing of the King by the Holy Spirit. This occurred at His baptism (3:13–17), when Jesus identified Himself with God's people, Israel—not because of a personal need for repentance. He had come as an Israelite, was circumcised in conformity with Jewish law, and now intensified His identification with Israel by participating in their baptism unto repentance. His anointing was His divine investiture into the Messianic office, the confirmation of heaven that He is the expected King.

Matthew tells the whole story of Jesus' temptation by Satan, for Satan was the usurper of the kingdom of this world—called "prince of this world." In the temptation, Satan offered Jesus the kingdoms of this world if only He would acknowledge him in worship, thus giving Satan the real sovereignty. It was the Kingdom that was at issue, as well as the sinless integrity of the Lord Jesus Christ. The struggle was between the rightful King and the evil usurper.

Of greatest interest is the section (chapters 5–7) called the Sermon on the Mount, incorporating the Laws of the Kingdom, or at least a sample of them. So majestic is this section that it has been called by such titles as the Mandate of the Kingdom. Here we have a glimpse of the ethics of the Kingdom, and just as we might expect, it is absolute ethical law. It points to God's strict governance of His people in the earthly Kingdom. For all its majesty, the Sermon on the Mount is not repeated in the New Testament Epistles in any form. These matters having to do with the constitution of the Kingdom are strangely missing from the letters to the churches.

These laws of the Kingdom were set forth by Jesus just prior to His offer of Himself to the nation Israel as their King. In the Sermon on the Mount we have in briefest glimpse a picture of Jesus as King, governing from the place of kingly power and authority. Fourteen times in the Sermon, Jesus adds His own word of kingly authority to that of the Old Testament law: *But I say to you*. His words in the Sermon have to do with the character of those who will enjoy the blessings of the Kingdom, the experiences they will pass through while being fitted for that Kingdom, and the laws which will govern them during the earthly reign of the King. Even the prayer which Jesus invited His disciples to emulate, was a prayer for the coming of that Kingdom, and for that unique time when the will of God would be done on earth in the same manner and to the same degree as it is done in heaven. Now, since the divorce-and-remarriage passages are related to this ethical Mandate of the Kingdom, we shall return to the Sermon on the Mount in more detail later on when we consider the ethics of the Kingdom in relation to the grace principles which govern the Church in an evil world.

Matthew then turns to the credentials of the King in chapters 8 and 9. These credentials are found in the mighty miracles which show forth Jesus' supernatural power to reign. The miracles prove His power over nature, sickness, death, sin, and the hosts of evil.

Although all three Gospels record the sending of the Twelve to preach and do miracles in His name, only Matthew records the words: ". . . Go nowhere among the Gentiles . . . but go rather to the lost sheep of the house of Israel" (10:5, 6). It is to them, *them only,* that the Twelve are to preach the message: *The kingdom of heaven is at hand.* The Kingdom is being offered to the people of Israel, not to the Gentiles.

Now Matthew comes to the rejection of the King, chapters 11 and 12. Numerous proofs of Israel's rejection are set forth, and there follows our Lord's denunciation of the religious leaders of the nation. Matthew continues on to show the official and final rejection of Christ at His public entry into Jerusalem. One looks in vain for any further preaching of the "gospel of the kingdom" except in the Olivet Discourse (chapters 24 and 25) where the reference is to a future time.

Chapter 13 of Matthew depicts Jesus turning to parables, the subject matter of which is called "the secrets of the kingdom of heaven." Eldon Ladd's comment here is that the mystery, or secret, of the Kingdom is the coming of the Kingdom into history in advance of its apocalyptic manifestation at the end of the age. The new truth, now given to men by revelation in the Person and mission of Jesus, is that the Kingdom which is to come finally in apocalyptic power has in fact entered into the world in advance in a hidden form to work secretly within and among men who receive the Saviour. Jesus plainly says that He is speaking in parables now because, in full accord with Isaiah's prophecy, the nation has now rejected their King and will not be able to receive these truths (13:11–17).

Matthew next records a strange incident in chapter 15:21–28—the story of a Canaanite (Syrophoenician), Gentile woman. When she addressed Jesus as Son of David, He answered her not a word. Jesus said to her, "I was sent only to the lost sheep of the house of Israel" (v. 24). He refused her request, urgent as it was, because she was not of Israel. However, when she then addressed Him as Lord, Jesus healed her daughter immediately.

Chapters 16 through 19 portray how the Pharisees tested Jesus' claims, Peter's great confession of Jesus as Messiah, the announcement of the new thing, the Church, and the Transfiguration of Jesus in which He manifested His glory. In this section Jesus was asked for a sign, and He replied that the only sign would be that of Jonah (a reference to His resurrection), for this was the one sign that would authenticate His kingly Person for all time (16:4).

Chapters 21 through 23 record the official rejection of the King which occurred at the time of His public entry into Jerusalem, the first and only time He did this. Here again we have the fulfillment of prophecy.

Even the cleansing of the Temple in Matthew 21 must be seen as an act of the King. The parables which Matthew records following the Jerusalem narrative are all Kingdom parables, leading to the great discourse in chapters 24 and 25. Here we have the final great prophetic utterance of the King, a comprehensive outline of events to take place as this age draws to a close. This prophetic discourse is found nowhere else besides Matthew's Gospel. It points to the One who shall come in power and great glory to reign.

Only Matthew records the expression "the consummation of the age." This present age will be terminated by the return of Jesus Christ (Matthew 24:3), by the judgment of men (13:39 ff.), and when the righteous will be separated from the wicked (13:49). The same expression occurs in Jesus' promise to His disciples after His resurrection—the promise of His presence with them in the consummation of the age (28:20). Jesus' coming and judgment mark the division between the present age and the age to come. This present age is viewed as an age in which Satan has been permitted to exercise a tragic sway over mankind. Only the age to come will witness his destruction. The dual nature of Kingdom teaching is that the Kingdom of God is the future eschatological victory over Satan, yet it is also a present event. Both emphases play important roles in Jesus' teaching. And nowhere do we see the interplay quite so complexly as in Matthew's Gospel. This does not make our problem any easier.

Before Matthew is finished he gives an account of the death and resurrection of the King, ending with the Great Commission (28:16–20). Included are His words, "All authority in heaven and on earth has been given to me." This is not a note of redemption; this is a Kingdom note. But it is a command which stands at a crucial point in the Great Transition. This King, although rejected by Israel and leaving earth until that future time when He can return to establish His Kingdom, is now a Saviour. The doors of salvation are flung open for all who will enter. The end of Matthew's Gospel is the beginning of the new age in redemption history.

The Remarkable Difference of John's Gospel

C. H. Dodd rightly claims that if we can understand John, we shall know what early Christianity really was. An interesting observation is this: The Gospel most Jewish in character lays great emphasis upon the Kingdom and the Old Testament references to it. The Gospel most removed from a Jewish audience and influence has the least about the Kingdom, and Old Testament references to it. Furthermore, if it is now the Kingdom in a different form that is the center of emphasis for the Church, why didn't John talk about the Kingdom in its new form? The answer is simply that John did not lay stress upon the Kingdom at all, in any form, including the hidden form of its present partial manifestation.

So radically different is the Gospel which John composed that critics have sometimes assigned it to an extremely late date and to Gnostic origins. Now, what Bishop Robinson calls the "new look" retrieves this Gospel to its proper Christian sources and to a date toward the end of the first century, and later in time than the Synoptics. But the importance of such critical views is to underscore the common observation that John's Gospel indeed is different in content from the others. Yet it can hardly be maintained that John wrote a supplementary Gospel, accentuating what the others left out. John did not omit what he presupposed either. The more traditional supposition that John wrote to supplement the Synoptic picture of Jesus' life has been almost universally abandoned. The relatively few points of direct contact between the outline of John and that of the Synoptics really create more problems than they solve. True, one may grant minor editing which would account for breaks in sequence, and variant forms of the same words. Isolated portions of discourse also might be explained by a desire to preserve some traditional word without being able to find an ideal place to insert it; this is true of the divorce saying isolated in its insertion in Luke's Gospel. But more importantly, the outline of John shows a cohesiveness in the overall plan. John's message is different from that of the Synoptics for sure, but it is self-consistent, unified in its theological purpose, and clearly represents a different orientation than that of the Kingdom.

The very fact that John is classified as a Gospel presupposes its dealing with the ministry of Jesus, and that it is based on a tradition similar in character to the traditions behind the Synoptic Gospels. It is theology written in an historical cast. Paul, too, was a theologian of similar sophistication, yet he did not write his theology in the framework of Jesus' earthly ministry. John's is truly a Gospel, and a Gospel different from the others for the reason that he presents teachings which are relevant to the Church in this interim age of grace—not teachings which concern the future Kingdom. Nor is his emphasis upon the hidden form of the Kingdom in its partial manifestation now. So we are not to be misled into classifying the four Gospels as having the same message simply because they are Gospels, and when content analysis shows otherwise. This is not to say that John doesn't share in common with the Synoptics a certain body of material. This includes part of the ministry of John the Baptist, the cleansing of the Temple, the healing of the royal officer's son, the feeding of the five thousand, the anointing of Jesus, the entry into Jerusalem, and the general outline of the Last Supper, the Passion, death, and resurrection. With regard to the sayings of Jesus this would include many isolated verses. Still, this must not lead to an identification of the message of John with that of the Synoptics.

An increasing number of scholars think that John was not dependent upon either the Synoptics or their written sources, but upon independent sources. There is the possibility, of course, that among his sources one or two might have been sources that seem to lie behind the Synoptics. It is hardly credible to suppose that John was unfamiliar with the tradition which exhibits itself in the Synoptics, as if his different emphasis was for the reason of unfamiliarity. Not at all. This is no more acceptable than Bultmann's surmise that John borrowed from the Synoptic tradition in order to make his Gospel acceptable to the Church at large. F. F. Bruce comments wisely that it is good to consider what sources the evangelists may have used; it is better to consider what use they made of their sources.

Finally, we must reject the notion that John was the theologian par excellence, and that this accounts for the wholly different nature of his Gospel. Equally untenable is the suggestion that John represents a degree of sophistication adapted to an audience outside of Palestine. If, in fact, the Church is the Kingdom—a concept unknown to John's audience—would it not be incumbent upon John to interpret that central concept to them? Would he not be at special pains to enable such an audience to grasp what was the very heart of the Kingdom message for their times? Surely John would not have been guilty of such failure—not when he wrote under the inspiration of the Holy Spirit!

We can grant that the Synoptic Gospels are not of the same theological quality, but explain it on the contention that they are concerned with one fundamental message—the offer, rejection, postponement, and promise of the eschatological Kingdom. To those who say that John's intention was to produce a document not of history, but of faith, we reply that John is indeed historical, but historical in the sense that he is concerned not only with what happened, but also with the deepest meaning of what happened. If the deepest meaning of what happened concerned the exchange of a literal Kingdom for a spiritual one, or the replacement of an eschatological Kingdom with its present form, then John failed his task! But to write directly and theologically to and for the Church meant for John a different approach than that of the Kingdom. This accounts for the difference in his ethical approach as well. He does not concern himself with the Sermon on the Mount, nor with the radicalized ethic which attends an emphasis upon the Kingdom. This is further reason for pursuing the possibility that Kingdom ethics go through a metamorphosis when adapted to the Church in the Old Aeon.

John provides the clue to his purpose in writing when he says,

"Now Jesus did many other signs in the presence of the disciples, which are not written in this book; but these are written that you may believe that Jesus is the Christ, the Son of God, and that believing you may have life in his name" (John 20:30, 31). And if one were to seek to lead a person into saving faith, into "life in his name," it would be through the presentation of the *gospel of God's grace* in John, not from material in any or all of the Synoptic Gospels.

The relevant question is not: To whom did John write in his day?—but rather: What is the Holy Spirit saying through John to the Church in all ages? The materials were selected by John for his own purpose—this we would not for a moment deny. But in the sense of divine inspiration, they were selected by the Holy Spirit so that believers of all ages might read and distinguish those things which are distinguishable! It is the Holy Spirit who had different purposes in view. And we have seen that it is the difference between the Kingdom in its full eschatological manifestation over against the Church—the ethic that shall most perfectly prevail in that Kingdom over against the ethic that shall only partially prevail in the Church interim.

Some speak of "realized eschatology" in John, inferring that the expectation of a literal Kingdom on Jesus' part was mistaken, and that the Kingdom has reality, but only a present reality. In such a view, John then teaches that all the ends for which Christ came are now realized. But this is utterly unconvincing. It is not as though John were stripping off apocalyptic elements from Christian thought, thus purifying the Church's doctrine of false eschatological ideas which Jesus mistakenly held. Least of all can we suppose that John was unfamiliar with these elements. After all, he was the author of the Apocalypse, the Book of Revelation! Nor is it adequate to say that John was philosophical—an existentialist. The simpler and more natural solution is simply to note that John turned his knowledge and his competence under God's leading to give the Church a basic theology, but did not find it necessary or expedient to include Kingdom truth. The proper emphasis for the Church lies elsewhere, except for its Kingdom hope for the future. The redemptive nature of God's ethical dealing with His people is where the stress is placed. In a theological sense, John belongs with the Epistles more so than with the Gospels. He concentrates upon the saving and sanctifying benefits of Christ's First Coming, and also upon the ministry of the Holy Spirit—truths almost completely absent in the Synoptics. In John there is a constant contrast between two worlds—the one above and the one below. This is quite different from the contrast between the Kingdom present in a partial form and the Kingdom still to come. John's is a completely Christian theology; that of the Synoptics is in large part pre-Christian. And although the Synoptic Gospels were written well after the beginning of the Church Age, they do not appear to presuppose the history of the Church as John more certainly does. So from whatever angle we look at it, the Synoptics have to do with the Kingdom and Kingdom ethics; everything about them has an eschatological cast. John, along with the Epistles, has to do with the Church in the interim, and more with the ethic of grace. The Synoptics demonstrate the absolute nature of God's righteousness; John and the Epistles major in the redemptive aspects of God's dealing with His people—with realized forgiveness and renewed possibilities for living life as God ordered it.

In further proof of the great difference, take the miracles as presented in Matthew and in John. In Matthew, the miracles are primarily acts of power which accompany the breaking into time of the reign of God. They are not simply external proofs of Jesus' claims, although they are that indeed. More fundamentally, they are acts by which He establishes God's reign and defeats the reign of Satan. Many of the miracles attack Satan directly by driving out demons. Many more are healings of sickness which is associated with the reign of evil. The raising of individuals to life is an assault on death which is Satan's peculiar realm. Even the nature miracles, like the calming of the sea, are an attack upon the disorders introduced into nature by Satan. Some miracles symbolize the fulfillment of Old Testament prophecies. It is for these reasons that the miracles come before us in the Synoptics.

Quite differently in John, miracles serve another function; they do not have in view the reign of God or the Kingdom of God, and therefore are not presented as acts of power which authenticate the Kingdom. John makes no apparent connection between the miracles and the destruction of Satan's power. Rather, as he himself says, the emphasis is upon spiritual symbolism, that we "may have life in his name" (*see* John 20:30). These were miracle-signs pointing to the Deity of Jesus. The word *sign* is used of miracles in the Synoptic Gospels, but not in the same way as in John. John does not have in mind the powerful intervention of God at the end of the age—miracles which attend His judgment of mankind.

It may seem curious that John was the only Gospel writer among the three privileged disciples who saw Jesus transfigured on the Mount of Transfiguration. Yet he did not recount the glorious incident. Matthew, who was not present, did recount it. Just how do we account for this? In harmony with our present study, it might be said that this incident properly had to do with the authenticating of Jesus the King rather than pointing to Jesus the Saviour, and hence it is appropriate to the purpose of Matthew's Gospel, not John's.

In further demonstration of the difference between Matthew and John, let us take a prominent narrative that is present in all four Gospels. The ministry of John the Baptist was to the nation of Israel exclusively. He was the precursor or herald of the King. He preached righteousness and judgment, calling the nation to repentance and restoration of their covenant privileges in anticipation of the coming of their Messiah. In this connection he baptized individuals in a baptism of repentance. This is not Christian baptism! Note how his disciples were rebaptized as Christians (Acts 19). This ministry of baptism ceased soon after he designated Jesus as Messiah. His single message was: *Repent, for the Kingdom of heaven is at hand*. The symbols of the Baptist were those of judgment in the record of Matthew. "Even now the axe is laid to the root of the trees . . ." (Matthew 3:10). Previously he said to the Pharisees, ". . . You brood of vipers! Who warned you to flee from the wrath to come? Bear fruit that befits repentance, and do not presume to say to yourselves, 'We have Abraham as our father' . . ." (Matthew 3:7–9). Then the Baptist points to the coming of Jesus as Judge: "His winnowing fork is in his hand, and he will clear his threshing floor and gather his wheat into the granary, but the chaff he will burn with unquenchable fire" (Matthew 3:12). This entire depiction is congruous with the prophetic expectation of the Messiah-King who will judge His people in righteousness.

Now, what do we find when we encounter this same John the Baptist in John? What the Synoptics include is for the most part omitted, and what John contains is for the most part not in the Synoptics. Is John simply being supplemental? This is to miss the whole point! What John includes and omits is in perfect accord with his major purpose. The theme of judgment is missing altogether. But what the Baptist is heard saying is, "Behold the Lamb of God who takes away the sin of the world!" (John 1:29). In conformity with the ministry depicted in the Synoptics, John does say ". . . that he might be revealed to Israel" (v. 31). But this Gospel does not conclude the identification at this point, for John the Baptist is further heard to say, as reported in this Gospel alone, "And I have seen and have borne witness that this is the Son of God" (v. 34). It is not clear to scholars whether the words of John 3:34–36 are spoken by Jesus or the Baptist, but if they are the words of the Baptist, then once more we find him relating his message to the offer of salvation to all. In this case, his message was not confined to the Kingdom as recorded in the Synoptics. From this example we further conclude that the Kingdom message of the Synoptics is largely eschatological and distinctly pre-Christian for the most part.

In the seventeen times it is found, *eternal life* in John's Gospel is the present possession of the believer, possessed on the basis of faith alone. In no sense whatever is it an ethical development. In contrast, the language of the Synoptics is "enter life," or "inherit life"—language similar to that for entrance into the Kingdom. The way of salvation by grace, by believing in the Lord Jesus Christ as one's personal Saviour, receiving eternal life as a gift of God's pure grace—this is not clearly set forth in even one passage in the Synoptics. John, in sharp distinction, is in perfect harmony with the Epistles in his theology. This cannot be said of the Synoptics, a fact recognized by most scholars.

If one were to ask, "What must I do to inherit eternal life?" and turn to Matthew for the answer, he would find a single passage in that Gospel, Matthew 19:17 (or perhaps also 25:46). He would hear Jesus answer the rich young ruler, "Keep the commandments." Jesus then listed the commandments. When the young ruler said that he had kept all of these, Jesus continued, "Go sell what you possess and give to the poor" (*see* 19:16–21). This is not New Testament ground! Obviously, in this instance there was a block to the kind of obedience that Jesus demanded for this young ruler to be a candidate for the Kingdom of God then being set before him. To universalize this requirement to all instances where the question is asked, "What must I do to inherit eternal life?" would be a contradiction to the central message of salvation by grace which characterizes the New Testament. In similar fashion, to consult the ethical mandate in the gospel of the Kingdom without qualification as to its intended application during the interim of the Church Age, would be equally misleading. It is the author's contention that the final word and consideration in the matter of divorce and remarriage is not contained in the ethical mandate as it is set forth in the absolute form recorded in the Kingdom teachings of Jesus. It is qualified and applied in broader terms in accord with the principles of grace and realized forgiveness which come through in developed fashion in the Epistles.

It is fully understandable that John does not incorporate any of the Sermon on the Mount, and *not* for the reason that to do so would be redundancy. His emphasis is upon the ministry of the Holy Spirit within believers, even as the Epistles stress the work of the Holy Spirit in conforming the inward person to the life of Jesus. John and the Epistles stress the inward development of the ethical life, the corollary of which is the rule of grace as it applies to immature growth and actual failure. The advanced theology in contrast with the Gospels ought surely to be apparent! John's Gospel is as far as one could be from any hint of a new law to govern the Church, and it is not surprising at all that we find no teaching on divorce and remarriage in John. More and more the New Testament develops around the high ethical ideal which Jesus reaffirmed, but along with it a realistic understanding of human failure even among the redeemed. Practical solutions are brought in alongside the absolute ethical demands.

We have now surveyed the special character of the Synoptic Gospels, and especially Matthew's setting in which are located the two most important passages on divorce and remarriage. The context is quite different in these two, each having a particular significance of its own, and both removed from the ethical context of John's Gospel and the Epistles. The first of these two contexts is the Sermon on the Mount—commonly referred to as the ethical Mandate of the Kingdom. The other context is a debate between the Pharisees and Jesus in which the issue is the Mosaic Law—not at all a Christian context. Both of these contexts must be subject to detailed examination; this we shall attempt in the following two chapters.

6

The Kingdom Ethic in General

When we speak of the Kingdom ethic, we refer directly to the ethical sayings enunciated by Jesus and recorded for the most part in the Synoptic Gospels. Scholars have long recognized the distinctive characteristics of this ethic in contrast with the ethic of the Epistles generally. Jesus enunciated His ethic against the background of Israel's Mosaic legislation, often as an intensification of that ethic. It is not always apparent how His abiding ethic is to be separated from its application to the Mosaic legislation. But clearly He went beyond it, expanding and amplifying, correcting and superseding. But more particularly, Jesus attached His ethic to His teaching concerning the Kingdom. To understand the Kingdom is to understand the ethic. An ethical transition is clearly present in the ministry of Jesus, which looked back to the Mosaic Law, yet forward to the eschatological Kingdom. Admittedly it is not always easy to distinguish between what attaches to the old ethical administration of Israel, and what attaches to the new ethical administration of the Kingdom. The major features, however, are fairly clear.

We have gone to some length in this book to clarify the nature of the Kingdom. It might be added that in a few places the Kingdom bears the abstract meaning of *reign* or *rule*. But in both Old and New Testaments it also refers to a future apocalyptic order into which the righteous enter at the end of this age—an earthly Kingdom over which the returning King holds absolute sway, a Kingdom of peace and righteousness.

This is what we refer to as the *eschatological Kingdom*. Our problem is to identify the Kingdom ethic as belonging wholly to the actual reign of the King in the eschatological Kingdom, yet at the same time genuinely present in the reign of Christ as the spiritually present Lord in the lives of believers today. Regardless of the form under which the Kingdom ethic is administered, it will have in common the righteousness of God as its norm. But the form holds importance inasmuch as it is not legalistically applicable to the Christian believer in the same way as it shall be in the actualized Kingdom. As it is applicable to the Church today, it is ethical principle administered apart from its legal conditions and penalties. It is God's righteous demand administered within the context of grace, realized forgiveness, and renewal.

Early in the book we described the two aeons which make up redemptive history, the Old and the New. The Old Aeon represents the fallen world from the time of man's first sin until the establishment of God's Kingdom on earth. The New Aeon represents essentially and predominantly the Kingdom of heaven on earth, that apocalyptic Kingdom yet to come. But it is our observation here—thanks to the insights of Helmut Thielicke—that these two aeons overlap. Not merely do they intersect, but they overlap, a part of each aeon running concurrently with a part of the other. This overlap of the two aeons forms an interim period which incorporates elements of both, yet is different from either. This is the Church Age. The reality of both aeons is found in this segment of redemptive history. It is readily seen that this contributes to a complex set of relationships for the Christian living in the interim. It compels him to face an interim ethic which embraces the ethical norms of the Kingdom, while at the same time embracing the limitations and conditions of the Old Aeon. The diagram which follows is an attempt to visualize the three distinct ethical contexts which come before us in the New Testament.

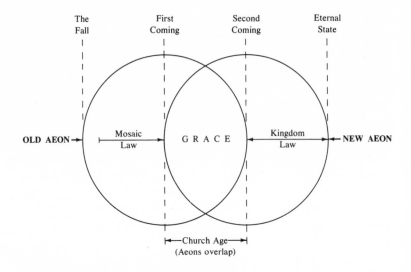

The Fall   First Coming   Second Coming   Eternal State

OLD AEON → ├── Mosaic Law ── G R A C E ── Kingdom Law ──┤ ← NEW AEON

├──Church Age──┤
(Aeons overlap)

    Inasmuch as the King and Kingdom were rejected by Israel, the consummated Kingdom is postponed until the King returns. Israel as a theocratic nation is set aside for the interim, and the Church has been formed to be the community of God's redeemed during this age. But the New Aeon is not contiguous to the Old, as though one simply followed the other. Inasmuch as the Old Aeon does not end until Christ comes to establish His Kingdom, yet because the Kingdom broke through in a partial manifestation with the First Coming of Christ, there is an overlapping of the two. Bridging the conditions of Old and New Aeons is the unique operation of God's redemptive grace. Because the King is absent except for His spiritual presence in the lives of believers, and because Satan is not yet bound and rendered inoperative in the world, only a partial fulfillment of the Kingdom ethic is possible. Failure shall mark the course of the Church Age. But such failure is not subject to the legal penalties of the Kingdom Law; judgment is not the necessary consequence. Redemptive grace is renewing grace, and realized forgiveness implies a restored potential for living in the fullness of God's design and blessing. It is this feature which makes the interim a distinct period in the ethical administration of God's righteous law.

So this age of grace is distinct unto itself as a form of God's rule. It is neither the Mosaic administration of theocratic law, nor is it the Kingdom administration of theocratic law. Life for the most part is governed by the principles of ethical appeal, along with the promise of the Holy Spirit's enabling. This is the characteristic feature of the Epistles which are addressed directly to the Church. The Church is not in any way a theocratic Kingdom; it is *in* the world but not *of* it or *over* it. The Church was not created to rule a universal society encompassing the nations of earth in a spiritual Kingdom. The Church is, if we may use the term, a subculture within the larger society of this world. Presently Satan is called "the god of this world" (2 Corinthians 4:4). He introduces disorder into human life in ways that affect Christian men and women, bringing conflict into human relationships. Inasmuch as God's people are not living in the perfectly realized form of the Kingdom, neither are they subject to a perfectly realized form of the Kingdom ethic. They can make only a relative response to this absolute Kingdom Law inasmuch as the supporting conditions of the Kingdom are not present—the universal rule of a present King, the power of Satan bound, and the divine execution of judgment upon transgressors in perfect justice. In the Kingdom of righteousness there shall be the more perfect fulfillment of God's righteous demands in the lives of His people. The crowning influence will be the presence of the Messianic King Himself in the power and glory of His reign. But until then, the conditions of the Old Aeon prevail throughout the interim, the Church struggles for its life in the world, and believers suffer the conflicts and contradictions of life in the world. Personal sanctification is realized in differing degrees in the lives of individual Christians, as growth in likeness of Christ is a progressive maturation in the Spirit. As Christian men and women differ both in their knowledge of God's will and in their ability to appropriate the resources available to them in Christ, there accordingly are degrees of failure in Christian experience. Christians find themselves in the sphere of limited fulfillment of the ethical ideal. There continues to be a conflict between the flesh and the Spirit (Galatians 5:16–24). As described in Romans 7, the regenerated person delights in the law of God with his mind, but he finds another law at war against this law. His continuing problem is that the conditions of the Old Aeon alter the possibility of fulfilling the law of the New Aeon.

At best, a Christian can only approximate the ideal. He is thus inextricably bound to the ethics of conflict and compromise, of failure and grace, of the tragic moral choice between the lesser of two evils. It is unknown to Christian experience that any redeemed person shall not face this experience in some area of life. The New Testament knows nothing of perfectionism. There is always a relative response to an absolute ethic, for this is the condition of man in the Old Aeon, even though the powers of the New Aeon have broken in upon him. But because this is the age of grace, the believer lives and moves and has his being in the sphere of realized forgiveness and redemptive restoration to life's highest possibilities. And although the present world order is anything but the realized Kingdom of God, Jesus did not pray that the Father would take His own out of the world, but that He would keep them from the evil one (John 17:15).

We see, then, that Christians stand in a relationship to both the Old and New Aeons—a relationship both of continuity and discontinuity at the same time. All too painfully do we recognize our continuity with the Old Aeon—succumbing at times to sins which so easily beset us, often coming short in Christian living. But there is a glorious discontinuity as well; believers are constantly being delivered from this evil age as they grow in Christ and in the power of the Spirit. The continuity with the New

Aeon is in a spiritual relationship with the living, indwelling Lord. Believers have "tasted the powers of the age to come" (*see* Hebrews 6:5). Yet, in the paradox of Christian life, discontinuity with the New Aeon is equally evident; the King and Kingdom are not presently established on earth, so an interim ethic is required for an interim age.

Christian ethics, as Thielicke has pointed out, is thus concerned with the Church's temporary ensconcement in this Old Aeon. The Christian ethic for this interim is decisively determined by this reality. God's will is that the fallen, passing world be respected as the real environment in which the Christian lives out his life in the Spirit. There is a cosmic struggle which touches life in this world. The problem of Christian ethics arises out of the tension between the continuity of life in this fallen world—and its accompanying discontinuity, and between the continuity of required obedience to Kingdom Law—and the discontinuity inherent in the fact that the conditions of the realized Kingdom are not present.

Christian ethics thus must be adapted to a field of tension. The Old Aeon is approaching its end, the New has already broken through in the coming and redemptive work of Christ. The New Aeon, while not our present environment, casts its ethical shadow upon our present history. It lays claim to us insofar as a partial fulfillment may be possible in this pre-Kingdom Age. In the few examples given in the Sermon on the Mount, for instance, we can see how Kingdom Law has radicalized the former Mosaic Law so as to adapt it to the new conditions of the Kingdom. Now the Christian must find a way to respond to this absolute law out of a relative capability made so by this Old Aeon.

Living in the field of tension between the two aeons, the Christian must recognize first of all that this tension cannot be resolved by attempting to perfectly fulfill a set of laws. Nor is it a matter of compromising God's absolute demands, inasmuch as those absolutes represent His unchanging character. No laws as such can satisfy both the continuity and discontinuity which we face in this world. Consequently, Christian ethics cannot aim to do away with the tension through compromises—supposedly doing justice to both elements in the tension thereby. Instead, Christian ethics must enable us to walk in both worlds, to live within the tension, to grow in personal responsiveness to the leading and empowering of God's Spirit, to discern the good and evil that lies beyond the parameters of law. At the same time, we draw guidance from Kingdom Law, appropriating it as rule, not as law. Ethical growth occurs, right within the tension and through imperfect fulfillment of the law's demands.

Thus it is that life in the interim Church Age, lived as it is in this field of tension, and amid imperfect fulfillments, is characterized by God's grace. What God requires He gives us in Christ. This is the life of growth, with imperfect yet realized fulfillments of God's righteous demand, with realized forgiveness in the face of failure, and with redemptive restoration to new possibilities. How vastly superior is this to any new law! Here is the mighty meeting of righteous demand and redemptive grace!

The ethic which governed the Old Aeon prior to the coming of Christ is no longer in force. The law of Moses was fulfilled in Him and no longer is the Mosaic legislation binding. It is done away forever in Christ. However, the moral precepts incorporated within the Mosaic Law are unchanging and are reaffirmed in the New Testament Epistles. But whereas under the Mosaic administration there was provision for penalty, not restoration, now under grace there is provision for restoration rather than penalty. This being the case, it is incumbent upon Christians to receive intact the requirement of God's absolute demands, seeking to fulfill them in the power of Spirit, all the while living provisionally under forgiveness and grace.

Kingdom Law bears witness to our existence as *de facto* sinners, albeit redeemed sinners with a new life in Jesus Christ. Thus, for example, the Sermon on the Mount protects us from the illusion that we are perfected, that we have achieved the norm of God's righteousness in earthly relationships. It continually says to us that we daily need the forgiveness and grace and restoration of God, that we must continually begin again when sin or failure has successfully intruded into our lives.

Now, God's law is not abolished, nor compromised in any way. God's law serves as the one ethical ideal to guide Christian decisions and conduct. It keeps before us the perfect standard of God's righteous demands upon all men at all times. But the law does not have dominion over us, and we are free from the curse of a broken law. Binding legal penalties are no longer the consequence of failure; grace has provided otherwise. God relates to the present fallen world by this incredible accommodation of His will which we call grace. In this accommodating grace God sustains this fallen world in the sphere of its remaining possibilities until the day of judgment. God acts toward mankind, not on the basis of His *unconditional will,* but upon His *conditional will*—His will altered for the sake of man in his incapacity.

Admittedly, God's present accommodation to this fallen aeon cannot be intrinsically justified, but exists only by divine patience and grace. Only His forgiving, restoring grace makes it possible. The very coming of Jesus Christ, in fact, was the Great Accommodation; this is triumphant grace! And now in this interim Church Age, grace triumphs amid the failures of God's people. This is the age of Redemptive Realism in the fullness of God's grace! Expositions of Kingdom Law in the Synoptics do not carry with them the disclosure of this Redemptive Realism, but this is introduced to us most fully in the Epistles. And this holds true of the question of divorce and remarriage. In this matter, as in all other relationships, the realized forgiveness of grace would be but a truncated reality did it not include full restoration to life's highest possibilities in God's creative design! This we shall see displayed most happily in the matter of marital failure, divorce, and remarriage.

Although the Christian is in position to appropriate the mighty power of the Holy Spirit, he is ever aware of being somewhat in bondage to his old nature of sin. He is still in the process of "putting off the old man" (*see* Ephesians 4:22; Colossians 3:9). There is the intersecting of the old and new natures within him. Sanctification is a progressive putting off of the old man and putting on of the new, of gradual conformity to the likeness of Christ. Although the Christian is a new creature in Christ, he is at the same time in the process of being delivered from the power of the unredeemed within himself. The pride of self and the passions of the flesh remain to be subjected to the lordship of Christ.

Helmut Thielicke reminds us that law always relates to the fallen nature of man—even that of redeemed man. This, of course, does not restrict law to the Old Aeon, but means the necessity for law in the Kingdom Age as well. For the Kingdom includes not only the redeemed but the unredeemed; it is a dual constituency that Scripture depicts. The moral life of the Kingdom shall be safeguarded by explicit divine sanctions, but it will be the redeemed governing the unredeemed. The ultimate transition from the earthly Kingdom to the eternal state will be immediate; employment of the law will no longer be required. But the eschatological Kingdom will be governed by law even as it will include God's exercise of grace.

That which distinguishes the Kingdom Age uniquely will be righteous judgment—the administration of justice on earth. This implies the employment of law for social order. There shall then be a very literal fulfillment of the prayer our Lord instructed His disciples to pray, "Thy kingdom come, Thy will be done, On earth as it is in heaven" (Matthew 6:10). But let us make no mistake—that will shall be done on earth according to Kingdom Law. This is perfectly clear in the mandate of the Sermon on the Mount.

A simple formula enables us more easily to distinguish *Kingdom teachings* from *grace teachings* in the New Testament: When human obligation is first required, with divine blessing made dependent upon the faithful discharge of that obligation, the ethical character is that of law. But when divine blessing is first offered, with the human obligation following in the form of an appeal, the ethical character is that of grace. The life of the Christian is distinguished by the offer of blessing on the basis of faith alone, with God appealing to the regenerate person to then live out his redeemed state in obedience through love. Law, whether it be the former Mosaic administration or the coming Kingdom administration, always involves a legalistic works-righteousness. In contrast, grace involves an unconditional covenant of what God promises to do on behalf of those who receive it by faith, and does not involve a legalistic works-righteousness. Good works follow because there is the incentive born of grace. What is conditional in the New Covenant is that believers shall be rewarded for obedience, and shall suffer loss for disobedience. But life always has redemptive possibilities.

The social and ethical organization of any human society requires a legal basis. Order must prevail and norms must sustain that order. So laws are then developed to fit the conditions of the society in particular. Thus, Mosaic Law was entirely appropriate for Israel as a theocratic nation among pagan nations. Similarly, Kingdom Law shall be appropriate for the universal society on earth when Messiah personally reigns over all. The present ethical governance of believers, on the contrary, is more internal than external, more through the Spirit's direction than through law. So radical a change was this for the Jewish believers, who had grown up under the Mosaic administration of law, that we have several instances of strife with Judaizers mentioned in the New Testament record. They tried to insist upon a continuance of the Mosaic legislation.

We speak of the Church Age as the *age of grace,* but not for the reason that divine grace has not been exercised in past ages.

God has always exercised His grace toward man. The law only condemned sinful man, pointing him to the salvation God offered to faith. The works-righteousness required by the law led to universal condemnation, and to salvation by faith in a gracious God. Galatians is classic in this regard: "Now before faith came, we were confined under the law, kept under restraint until faith should be revealed" (Galatians 3:23). One is reminded of the summary statement in the prologue of John's Gospel: "For the law was given through Moses; grace and truth came through Jesus Christ" (John 1:17). Perhaps the most remarkable passage in this connection is Ephesians 2:7–9: "That in the coming ages he might show the immeasurable riches of his grace in kindness toward us in Christ Jesus . . . . the gift of God—not because of works . . . ." There evidently is to be a demonstration of divine grace in all its uniqueness and richness, a demonstration before all the creatures in God's cosmic population. The Church is the subject of that demonstration. How different is this demonstration of pure grace from what God ordered in the Mosaic administration of the past. Nor is it the same as that which He will do in the Kingdom administration yet to come. Nowhere is the rule of grace better summarized than in Paul's declaration:

> For the grace of God has appeared for the salvation of all men, training us to renounce irreligion and worldly passions, and to live sober, upright, and godly lives in this world, awaiting our blessed hope, the appearing of the glory of our great God and Savior Jesus Christ, who gave himself for us to redeem us from all iniquity and to purify for himself a people of his own who are zealous of good deeds.
>
> Titus 2:11–14

Here we have all the elements of the New Testament rule of life by grace, not law. Salvation is by grace without law; our ethical life develops as a matter of training in righteousness, not as a response to law. We are not commanded to do certain things and to omit doing other things as a matter of legal sanction, but rather that our lives are to be characterized by a certain quality, guided not by rules so much as by principles of conduct. The motivation to good deeds is positive, not negative—by the anticipation of our Lord's smile of approval, not the fear of legal sanctions. We live to please and glorify Him, to do His will. How utterly different, both in content and tone, is this rule of life in comparison with the legalistic ethic of the Kingdom yet to come.

The whole difference between these two ethical systems—law and grace—is stressed in several phrases found in 2 Corinthians 3:6: ". . . not in a written code but in the Spirit; for the written code kills, but the Spirit gives life." More precisely, Romans 7:6 reads: "But now we are discharged from the law, dead to that which held us captive, so that we serve not under the old written code but in the new life of the Spirit." Romans 6:14 reads: ". . . since you are not under law but under grace." Of course, to be under grace also places a high ethical demand upon the believer, as Paul continues in this same passage:

> What then? Are we to sin because we are not under law but under grace? By no means! Do you not know that if you yield yourselves to any one as obedient slaves, you are slaves of the one whom you obey, either of sin, which leads to death, or of obedience, which leads to righteousness? But thanks be to God, that you who were once slaves of sin have become obedient from the heart to the standard of teaching to which you were committed, and, having been set free from sin, have become slaves of righteousness.

Romans 6:15–18

The purpose of the Holy Spirit's ministry to Christians is to produce, not law keepers as such, but lives that are more and more Christlike within and without. Note the characterization of this life in terms of the fruit of the Spirit: "But the fruit of the Spirit is love, joy, peace, patience, kindness, goodness, faithfulness, gentleness, self-control; against such there is no law" (Galatians 5:22, 23). How different is this from categories of legal requirements! This points to personal character and conduct over against external conformity to law.

Of great significance is the observation that grace teachings were not hinted at in the Old Testament at all, and are nowhere disclosed in the Synoptic Gospels. For what reasons? Principally because it required the descent and indwelling presence of the Holy Spirit to render effectual such a life in grace. Now, since Pentecost, ethical guidance and the empowerment of the Holy Spirit are sufficient to direct the Christian in every life situation.

A characteristic feature of the rule of grace in the Church interim is the use of appeal along with command. (*See* Romans 12:1 and Ephesians 4:1 as examples.) In these grace appeals there is an element missing that is common to the ethical mandates of both Mosaic and Kingdom Law. It is the legal element of judgment. The Kingdom commands hold out the danger of hellfire for failure of observance (Matthew 5:22, 29, 30). But quite to the contrary, the gloriously transcendent message of grace is: "There is therefore now no condemnation for those who are in Christ Jesus" (Romans 8:1). Although the Old Testament prophets foretold the swift judgment that would be incurred by the transgressor during the Kingdom (Isaiah 2:1–4; 11:1–5), God also promised His people that He would put His laws in their minds and write them on their hearts (Jeremiah 31:31–40; Hebrews 8:7–12). This speaks of divine assistance, of God enabling His people to keep what He has commanded. So here in this description of the Kingdom Age, the elements of law and the enabling power of the Holy Spirit are combined.

The utter impossibility of perfect righteousness under the Old Testament law is the same utter impossibility of perfect righteousness in the present age, before the actual coming of the Kingdom. Yet a part of God's gracious provision is to declare what Kingdom righteousness is and what it demands, pointing us in the one proper ethical direction. It serves as the ethical ideal or goal, and in the power of the Holy Spirit we are to seek to realize at least a partial fulfillment. To the degree that we are enabled to rise higher by God's Spirit, to that same degree we experience the joy of His righteousness and blessing. To that degree, Christian life is lived to God's glory. This, of course, is far from saying that the Kingdom mandate is a new law for the believer today. It is not law at all. Nor is it to say that believers shall be penalized for only partially fulfilling the law—that is, for partial *un*fulfillment of the law.

The enabling power of the Holy Spirit is unlimited in itself, even in this Old Aeon. However, man's ability to appropriate His power is limited by the degree of individual growth in Christ and knowledge of His will. Nor can he escape altogether from the powers of this fallen age. For this reason, quite paradoxically, it can be said that the righteousness of the Kingdom is presently both attainable and unattainable; it is attainable in part but not in fullness. It is both practical and impractical; it is indeed for this age, yet not for this age. It is the "impossible possibility." What is attainable for some is not attainable for all. This, we shall see, has great bearing on the problem of marital failure among Christians.

It is this realism that must come to prevail in the thinking of the Church today. Where, actually, can the Church point to ethical perfection within its life in the world? And if not elsewhere, then assuredly not in the most intimate and demanding relationship of all—marriage. Rather, the Church is called upon to exercise the same grace toward marital failure that God exercises toward whatever failure His children suffer. And where sin is involved, there is forgiving grace, too.

In this aeon, Satan is eager to bring testing upon God's people, constantly aiming to frustrate the working of Kingdom principles among God's own. We cannot underestimate the power of Satan in this age. But when the Kingdom is inaugurated with the coming of the King, then Satan will be first bound and then later destroyed, but not until then. This, we conclude, is the problem of the theology of the Synoptic Gospels for the Church of the interim: the Kingdom of God is the future end-time victory over Satan, yet it is also a present realizable victory in the lives of the redeemed. This present possibility, however, is within the limitations of the Old Aeon and the conditions imposed by the world, the flesh, and the devil. Thus God brings in advance of the end-time the blessings of His redemptive reign in part. It is in this sense that we understand the proper translation of Matthew 12:28: ". . . the kingdom of God has come upon you." The signs and powers of the Kingdom are manifested in a real though limited way. Jesus brought a foretaste of the Kingdom, and He continues to do so within the experience of His own. But it is only that—a foretaste.

One of the main tasks of the Church in the world is to display to this present evil age the life and fellowship of the age to come. For while the Church in this age will never attain ethical perfection—and this will be conspicuous in such areas as marital failure—it must nevertheless display the life of that perfect order as it breaks through in the power of God's Spirit. Despite failures, there will be many instances of realized victory. In this way the Church witnesses to that coming Kingdom and demonstrates its reality.

We can agree with a host of scholars, both conservative and liberal, who conclude that the ethics of Jesus are Kingdom ethics set entirely within an eschatological context. Men as diverse as E. F. Scott and Paul Ramsey concur that Jesus' ethic was totally conditioned by eschatology, setting forth the will of God for life in the eschatological Kingdom. Eldon Ladd summarizes by saying that if Jesus' ethics are in fact the ethics of the reign of God, it follows that they must be absolute ethics. Dibelius is right, says Ladd: Jesus taught the pure, unconditional will of God, without compromise of any sort, which God lays upon men at all times and for all time. Such conduct is actually attainable only in the age to come when all evil has been banished. But it is quite clear, too, from the Sermon on the Mount that Jesus expected His disciples to practice His teachings in this present age, even as they anticipated the coming of that future Kingdom. The Kingdom has entered history, but without transforming history. And during this time of waiting, it is an imperfect Church that readily confesses its imperfection, yet points to the incredible grace of God. It is the God of all grace who is in the business of mending broken lives, and nothing delights Him more than to restore to new possibilities those who have failed. He says to those who have failed but come to Him, "Neither do I condemn you; go, and do not sin again." (*See* for a clear example of this, John 8:11.) In such ethical concerns as divorce and remarriage, it is really to the God of all grace that we should look, not alone to the absolute ethical law and the particular Kingdom conditions under which it shall be in fullest force.

7

The Sermon on the Mount in Particular

The declaration of Jesus concerning divorce and remarriage in chapter 5 of Matthew has special significance for the reason that it is in the Sermon on the Mount. It is thus a part of the highest ethical mandate to come from the lips of Jesus. It would seem on the face of it that this is sufficient reason to adopt this declaration as God's ultimate word to His people in any age. Nothing could be more misleading, although this has been, and continues to be, the traditional response to this passage of Scripture. And this has been true from the Patristic Age on. But the Sermon on the Mount is the very heart of Kingdom teaching. It is the Manifesto of the King, the legal Mandate of the Kingdom. It authenticates His kingly authority, and the transcendence of Kingdom Law over Mosaic Law. Jesus shows that He stands above the law as given by Moses and interpreted by Israel's leaders. A new degree of righteousness is attached to the conditions which will obtain in the Messianic Kingdom. More than one third of the Sermon is dominated by eschatology, including the Beatitudes and the warnings. It is legitimate to say that our Lord's whole teaching in the Sermon on the Mount has an eschatological background. It is completely contingent upon the coming of the Kingdom in its fullness.

Look at the simple declarations and direct commandments of the Sermon; is this not legalism for the most part? Is this not ethical perfectionism quite beyond all present human capability and expectation? Is this not, indeed, every bit as much an obedience-ethic as the Mosaic Law—only greatly intensified? Nothing is said here about man's inability to perfectly obey, nothing about the saving grace of the Saviour, and nothing at all about the Holy Spirit as the needed Enabler. There is no reference whatever to the new relationships which belong to those who are the New Creation in Christ. It is purely a righteousness attained by right inward attitudes and outward obedience. *It is law, not gospel!* The Sermon on the Mount stands fully in line with the Old Testament law in the sense that law endlessly repeats: *Obey and you will live!* Some commentators say that the Sermon on the Mount presupposes regenerate persons, but this really doesn't satisfy the questions raised by the works-obedience aspect. Jesus addresses the pure will of God to the responding will of man. Whereas Paul affirms the need for a transformed will, the Sermon affirms only the need for an exertion of will—presupposing this to be a human possibility on man's own. Hans Windisch sees two kinds of ethical teaching standing side by side: eschatological ethics conditioned by the expectation of the coming Kingdom, and noneschatological ethics. He insists that these are really foreign to each other. The predominant ethics are eschatological—the new demands for entrance into the Kingdom. Their radical character is conditioned by the absolute will of God without reference at all to man's predicament through sin and incapability. He says, "The religion of the Sermon on the Mount is predominantly a religion of works." He also makes the comment: "There is a gulf here between Jesus and Paul that no art of theological exegesis can bridge." Windisch expresses what many have wrestled with, namely, the ethical gulf that exists between the radical ethic of the Kingdom, and the New Testament Epistles' approach through grace principles.

The Sermon on the Mount is a collection of sayings brought

together in one discourse. Jesus is pictured as the new Moses on the mountaintop of ethical declaration. The sayings cover three entire chapters in Matthew—the Gospel of the Kingdom and the King. The Sermon on the Mount is found nowhere else, although there are parallels in the Sermon on the Plain in Luke 6:17–46. The Kingdom is mentioned eight times in the Sermon, and clearly this is the eschatological orientation of the ethic being enunciated.

The Kingdom message opens with the Beatitudes, the record of the ninefold blessing which is promised to the faithful child of the Kingdom (Matthew 5:3–12). The very first Beatitude mentions the Kingdom of heaven. The blessings mentioned are earned by the attitudes and acts enjoined. How striking is the contrast with the ninefold blessing which is said to be produced in the Christian by the ministry of the Holy Spirit (Galatians 5:22, 23). What is here demanded by the law of the Kingdom as a condition of blessing is provided under grace. Of course, while this is directly a part of Kingdom teaching, each of the qualities of spiritual life and action enjoined is a picture of the righteousness which the pure will of God demands. As such it should speak to every Christian, although he receives it for himself as the simple way of righteousness, not that which will earn him a reward.

If there is a summary statement in the Sermon on the Mount which discloses the essential nature of its message, it is Matthew 5:20: ". . . unless your righteousness exceeds that of the scribes and Pharisees, you will never enter the kingdom of heaven." There it is, all of it, in capsule form—as though Jesus were saying: "You talk of righteousness by the law of Moses; I'm telling you of the true righteousness of God which supersedes the law of Moses. The righteousness of Messiah's Kingdom is internal as well as external, and it is no less perfect. If a man would claim righteousness, he must be as righteous as God, for there is no righteousness which brooks the divine standard. If a man would come to God on the basis of his own righteousness, let him know that God neither knows nor accepts any righteousness other than perfect righteousness.''

The whole thrust of the Sermon is about that righteousness which exceeds that of the scribes and Pharisees. It should remove the illusion of superior righteousness which had hold upon the Pharisees. While it remained the central aspect of apostolic preaching that there is no righteousness by the law, Jesus did not go into this at all in the Sermon. He is explicating the nature of righteousness by law, and showing how the Mosaic Law shall be intensified by the Kingdom Law. And if one were to notice, Jesus only presented five subjects, not in their independent significance, but rather as examples to express and document what the Kingdom shall be like, nothing more.

A crucial point is made in Matthew 5:17: "Think not that I have come to abolish the law and the prophets; I have come not to abolish them but to fulfil them." He is about to reinterpret the law of Moses, viewing it in its lofty internal dimensions, and thus intensifying its demand. Quite clearly, this intensifying of the law is due to the Kingdom expectation. The law has a higher relation to Kingdom righteousness. Even condemnation for failure is intensified: "Whoever then relaxes one of the least of these commandments and teaches men so, shall be called least in the kingdom of heaven . . . ." (v. 19). Interestingly, there is nothing comparable to this in the Epistles, which govern Christian life in the Spirit. Jesus here shows His relationship to Mosaic Law. He came under this law and lived by this law, and authenticates His right to reinterpret the law at a level unknown to the nation Israel. That the Kingdom is on a higher plane of law keeping is evident immediately when He adds, "For I tell you, unless your righteousness exceeds that of the scribes and Pharisees, you will never enter the kingdom of heaven" (v. 20). The whole orientation is to the Kingdom of heaven and qualifications attaching thereto. It requires a superior righteousness, but a righteousness nonetheless related to the law as they have known it. Then follow six examples of the way Jesus reinterprets the law. Each is opened with the words, "You have heard that it was said . . . ." Then He adds to the example of the law, "But I say to you . . . ." He shows how the law shall be elevated to new demands in the Kingdom. So serious is Jesus about the true demands which the law shall impose in the Kingdom, that He resorts to hyperbole in the statement, "If your right eye causes you to sin, pluck it out and throw it away; it is better that you lose one of your members than that your whole body be thrown into hell" (v. 29). This idea is repeated, this time, "And if your right hand causes you to sin . . ." (v. 30). The idea behind the use of hyperbole is clear enough. Yet how strange this is to the Christian who is familiar with God's provision for the problem of sinning expounded in the Epistles. The post-Calvary assurance is in 1 John 1:9.

The divorce-and-remarriage passage (vv. 31, 32) consists of one of these six examples of the superior righteousness of the Kingdom which Messiah shall establish on earth. Jesus radicalizes the law of Moses, and here no less than with the other Mosaic orders. This time He removes a provision, the Mosaic provision for divorce (*see* Deuteronomy 24:1–4). He shows that in the Kingdom the provisions made for the "hardness of man's heart" shall no longer obtain. A higher standard shall be enforced. Thus, along with the superior blessings of the Kingdom Age, there shall also be superior demands. As for Christians, the legal aspect inculcated in these six examples does not concern them; what does concern them is the way of righteousness which they should seek to make their own. The consequences of failure are not the same, if we read the Epistles aright—there is no penalizing effect in the rule of grace. On the other hand, the Sermon does not concern itself with the redemptive solutions which attend Christian failures. It is concerned with judgment, not forgiving and renewing grace. This shows it to be outside the pale of the post-Calvary message of the New Testament. Christians can gain no teaching about divorce and remarriage from this passage in the context of the Kingdom other than to support the ethical ideal that marriage is to be enduring, not necessitating divorce. Beyond that we cannot carry the Kingdom Law into Christian ethics.

To cap the whole essence of Jesus' sayings in the Sermon on the Mount, listen to the closing sentence in this section of chapter 5: "You, therefore, must be perfect, as your heavenly Father is perfect" (v. 48). Numerous and divergent interpretations have been given to this statement. The key to it all is the word *perfect*. We grant the possibility of alternate meanings, but the context urges upon us the consistent thought that the righteousness of God is pure and perfect. He speaks to us in absolutes —though our response can only be made in a relative way. God never lowers the level of divine righteousness to its human accommodations. If one is to be righteous before God, it must be perfect righteousness. Jesus thus leaves his hearers in the tension between the absolute, pure will of God, and the problem of human obedience. As He offers the Kingdom to Israel, He makes it clear that the Kingdom shall be governed in righteousness, including the law of marriage. Israel knew well what it was to accept or reject. Everything in the Sermon, quite obviously, is not Kingdom Law. There is an intermingling of teaching for discipleship that is universally adaptable. Jesus includes the promises and encouragements which also accompany the life of the Kingdom. These, too, have their applications to Christians in this age.

What a contrast between Jesus' warning: "For I tell you, unless your righteousness exceeds that of the scribes and Pharisees, you will never enter the kingdom of heaven," with the words in Titus 3:5–7: "He saved us, not because of deeds done by us in righteousness, but in virtue of his own mercy, by the washing of regeneration and renewal in the Holy Spirit, which he poured out upon us richly through Jesus Christ our Savior, so that we might be justified by his grace, and become heirs in hope of eternal life.'' The first has to do with entrance into the Kingdom of heaven by human righteousness; the second has to do with salvation apart from deeds done by us in righteousness. The first says nothing at all about God's mercy or grace; the second says it is all "in virtue of his own mercy." The first says nothing about regeneration, or renewal in the Holy Spirit, or the saviourhood of Jesus, or justification by His grace; the second includes all of these essential aspects.

By midpoint in the Sermon we come to the prayer our Lord taught His disciples to pray (Matthew 6:9–13). This is most commonly called the Lord's Prayer, and has been ritualized into the Sunday services of countless churches that hold to the Reformation view of the Kingdom as to be fully present in the Church. But this is not, strictly, the "Lord's Prayer," but rather a prayer Jesus taught the disciples to pray at a particular point in His ministry. The true "Lord's Prayer" is found in the seventeenth chapter of John's Gospel, and is nothing at all like the prayer we are here considering. This prayer in Matthew was appropriate to pray when Jesus and His disciples contemplated the Kingdom as a present possibility then being offered to Israel. It is a model prayer for those who were expecting the imminent establishment of the Messianic Kingdom on earth. The first supplication is, "Thy kingdom come, Thy will be done, On earth as it is in heaven." (v. 10). Now—of course—we, too, can pray in like manner for the Kingdom to come and for God's will to be done on earth as it is in heaven. We, too, expect the return of the King for this purpose. But clearly Jesus meant the coming Messianic Kingdom. He did not mean, "Thy Kingdom grow from these beginnings," nor could He have meant, "May Thy present Kingdom be perfected." Much less would the disciples have understood Him to mean, "Thy true Kingdom is spiritual; may it so develop in the hearts of mankind." Nothing of the sort! Jesus is consistent in referring to the Kingdom promised to Israel, and to all nations through Israel. The disciples would have understood a literal Kingdom. Messiah was in their midst, and He was announcing at that time, "The Kingdom of heaven is at hand." That Kingdom was not yet present, only "at hand," and it was for its coming that the disciples were to pray. That God's will should be done on earth was part of the expectation concerning His Kingdom reign on earth. It required the Messianic rule to bring about the will of God on earth; the two parts of this petition are inseparable.

At the close of the prayer, some ancient authorities add, "For thine is the kingdom and the power and the glory, for ever. Amen." Our Lord does not presently rule in His Kingdom, nor does He manifest His power and glory on earth as He shall in that day. God's will is not done on earth as it is in heaven, nor is it being done to any greater extent now than it has in centuries past. The will of God is locked in conflict with the self-centered and disobedient will of mankind.

This prayer was entirely harmonious with the burden of Jesus' ministry at the time. It is a prayer which has elements in common with the major concerns of the Church today, but some elements which are not directly applicable. You do not find a prayer of this nature either in John's Gospel or in the Epistles. If one were to compare the prayers of Paul with this prayer, one would be more impressed with the dissimilarities than similarities. Did not the great apostle learn from this prayer which our Lord instructed His disciples to pray? This really isn't the point. Christian concerns are different in scope and in their central direction. When this is not understood, how confused are the supplications of this prayer with the concerns and conditions of grace!

The chief example of this confusion is the petition: "And forgive us our debts, As we also have forgiven our debtors" (v. 12). In much the same fashion as the Beatitudes which appear earlier in the Sermon, this petition speaks as though the blessing of forgiveness were contingent upon one's claim to having forgiven others. Were this in any doubt, the words which follow the prayer make it perfectly plain: "For if you forgive men their trespasses, your heavenly Father also will forgive you; but if you do not forgive men their trespasses, neither will your Father forgive your trespasses" (vv. 14, 15).

Now, it may be argued that this has nothing to do with the forgiveness of salvation, but is a practical matter of experiencing forgiveness. For ourselves, the prayer is found within the ministry of Jesus in its earliest phases, when quite clearly He was offering the Kingdom and dealing with matters relevant to its coming. This petition is a further extension of Kingdom ethics, a legal approach to forgiveness which is totally unlike the passages on forgiveness which one confronts in the Epistles. How different is the approach of grace! For example, in Ephesians 4:32 we read, ". . . forgiving one another, as God in Christ forgave you." It is the forgiveness which God has given us that is the basis for Paul's appeal for us to forgive in like manner. (*Compare* Colossians 3:13 and 1 John 1:9.)

This model prayer for Kingdom concerns is most noteworthy for the absence of concerns central to believers in the Church Age. There is no note of thankfulness or praise for God's provision of salvation by grace, for redemption accomplished, for life empowered by the Spirit. Nor is there any petition for the unsaved, for the welfare of the Church in the world, or for the overcoming of Satan's power. This is strictly a prayer for the disciples to pray during the ministry of Jesus as He offered the Messianic Kingdom. It is pre-Christian—and that it contains Christian elements in no way alters the fact. The point we make once again is that there are elements in the Sermon on the Mount which belong to the Kingdom and not to the Church. We need discernment in making applications so that some principles are retained for their universality, while the more specific Kingdom applications are left to their own sphere.

In the last third of the Sermon, two statements stand out as illustrative of the Kingdom orientation of the whole. Matthew 7:12 has Jesus say, "So whatever you wish that men would do to you, do so to them; for this is the law and the prophets." Here the legal nature of the Kingdom is displayed once again, and its ties with the Mosaic period declared. There is nothing here of grace. The second statement in this last third of the Sermon, to which we might point as illustrative of the Kingdom orientation, is 7:13, 14: "Enter by the narrow gate, for the gate is wide and the way is easy, that leads to destruction, and those who enter by it are many. For the gate is narrow and the way is hard, that leads to life, and those who find it are few." This cannot possibly remind any New Testament reader of the conditions set forth by our Saviour and recorded by John regarding entrance into eternal life! It is not by a narrow gate but the wide arms of grace. The parallel passage in Luke 13:24 begins with the words, "Strive to enter by the narrow door . . . ." Nowhere is the Christian told that he must strive to enter into his salvation heritage! There is a world of difference between striving and believing!

The Kingdom Law, it is to be noted, is absolutely unyielding. For example, "Judge not, that you be not judged. For with the judgment you pronounce you will be judged, and the measure you give will be the measure you get" (7:1, 2). But the Christian has passed beyond judgment in his position in Christ (John 5:24). There is, of course, temporal judgment for Christians for the sake of their chastening, but this is not of the nature of sin returning upon them (*see* 1 Corinthians 11:32). And for the Christian, confession is the way indicated for forgiveness and cleansing (1 John 1:9).

The Sermon on the Mount concludes, not with gracious promises but with warnings. It is stated in Matthew 7:13–23 that only the few, only the most dedicated and obedient will achieve the way that leads to life. Finally, the final section reaches its climax in the contrast of verses 24 to 27: "Every one then who hears these words of mine and does them will be like a wise man who built his house upon the rock . . . . And every one who hears these words of mine and does not do them will be like a foolish man who built his house upon the sand . . . ." Here everything hinges upon the doing of the commands. The few, by strenuous effort, will achieve obedience; the rest may strive, but will fall. And so it is that the Sermon on the Mount is law, not grace. It is the Mandate of the Kingdom, not the road map of the Church. It contains principles which are applicable to the Church Age, but it also contains elements which belong only to the Kingdom. In our consideration of divorce and remarriage it should be noted that the words of Jesus in the Sermon on the Mount contain a prohibition which, when broken, is tantamount to adultery. This is the strict law of the Kingdom; it is transcended in the grace approach of the Epistles to the Church. The ethical goal is clear: marriage without divorce. Beyond this ideal we may not press the passage to serve our Christian concern. We look rather to the teachings of grace, realized forgiveness, and renewal of life's possibilities in the Spirit to gain a fuller understanding of how to regard marital failure and God's best for those involved.

Now, to bring together the Kingdom ethic in general with the Sermon on the Mount in particular, and to summarize how God's will is administered in the Mosaic, Church, and Kingdom Ages.

We've noted three ethical administrations of God's will within man's redemptive history. The three periods are the Mosaic, Church, and Kingdom Ages. These three are related in special ways, yet separate and distinct. The Kingdom Age was to have been the fulfillment and successor to the Mosaic. However, the Kingdom offer was rejected by Israel, and the Kingdom postponed until a yet future time, awaiting the return of the King. In the interim, God continues His redemptive program, calling all men to faith in Christ as their personal Saviour. Since the Church is neither a theocratic nation such as Israel, nor the promised universal Kingdom, it is not governed by law but by grace. One feature prevails in all three administrative modes: God's pure will is made conditional by the conditions of the Old Aeon. And each of God's administrative modes is appropriate to the age in which it functions.

By God's conditional will, we mean His grace-motivated accommodation to a fallen world in which His people must live and move and have their being. With respect to His own people, this accommodation of grace takes into account the degrees of sanctification represented by individual believers. God's will is absolute and unchanging, but it is made subject to His sovereign choice to manifest His grace to a sinning world. Grace, then, conditions God's will by providing full and free forgiveness, by renewing life's possibilities on the basis of Christ's atoning work. The conditional will of God expresses His expectation that redeemed men and women cannot, under the conditions of this age, reach perfect righteousness. Man's response to God's absolute will shall always be relative, a partial fulfillment at best. The redeemed person stands continually within the forgiving grace of God in Christ. This is what it means to be "in Christ." Not that there is no expectation of major fulfillment of God's will; on the contrary, every provision has been made for Christian life to appropriate God's resources for spiritual and moral growth!

Somewhat paradoxically, then, we speak of God's absolute, unconditional will for man, while at the same time we speak of His conditional will which is administered in different modes. One time it is *law,* another *grace.* Under *law,* God acts graciously; under *grace,* God points to the law as the standard of His righteousness and as the goal of life in the Spirit. The different modes of administering His will correlate with the different provisions for man's enablement. Under Mosaic Law, God's people were left to the strength of their own desire and will. During the Church Age, a higher, more internal standard is placed before the redeemed. It demands an inward conformity to God's will rather than a response to law. But with the higher standard there is also provided the indwelling of the Holy Spirit; He is the dynamic power given for the fulfillment of God's will. The Christian's ethical posture is expressed in an increasing likeness to Jesus Christ both in personal and social dimensions. When we come to the Kingdom Age, the administration of God's conditional will undergoes yet another transmutation. Now the conditions of life are altered in an extraordinary way: the King is present to rule in majesty and power, all of earth's kingdoms are increasingly brought under His reign and the redeemed have been changed into His likeness to rule with Him in peace and righteousness. Law in the Kingdom Age is intensified and internalized; it is adapted to the higher demands of Kingdom rule. The enabling power of the Holy Spirit is even more apparent.

Jesus gave tacit acknowledgment to the changing administration of God's conditional will when He said to the Pharisees who questioned Him about the Mosaic divorce law, ". . . but from the beginning it was not so" (Matthew 19:8). From the beginning there was no provision for divorce in the administration of God's will, because man had not fallen into sin, and the administration of God's will was as yet unconditional. No need existed for such divine accommodation as sin later necessitated. Divorce simply did not fit the creative order of indissoluble marriage.

Under Moses, it was a different story—man was sinful and disabled from fulfilling God's absolute will. Whenever he failed, there had to follow either divine judgment or divine grace. Even within the severity of the law, God's conditional will is seen in His permission for divorce and remarriage. As a concession to man's weakness and failure, this was an expression of God's grace. (Deuteronomy 24:1–4 sets forth the Mosaic concession of divorce.)

In the interim Church Age of grace, there is not a lesser accommodation to man's weakness and failure. Conditions for failure are all the greater, even as God's provision for success is greater. The provision for divorce and remarriage simply is no longer in the context of *law* but of *grace*. The seriousness of it can be measured by the law of the Kingdom which Jesus announced. But it is presently not a matter of legal sanctions and status; it is a matter of realized forgiveness and renewal of life's possibilities.

Now, to say all this is not to relativize the demands of the Sermon on the Mount. On the contrary, we take the absoluteness of its requirements with utter seriousness; the Holy Spirit will so direct the Christian conscience. It is simply that we recognize that this aeon is the sphere of relativities, of man's less-than-perfect ability, and of God's continuing grace. Divorce and remarriage do not correspond to the pure intention of God—they cannot. Rather, they ever stand as concessions of divine grace to the "hardness of men's hearts" (*see* Matthew 19:8). This condition sometimes makes divorce inevitable. In such a world where even Christians are caught up in the tangled web of human relationships, God causes the grace of His accommodating intervention to triumph over even the legitimacy of His original claim upon a couple. Of course, we misunderstand this divine accommodation completely if we regard it as a license for complicity with the forces of this evil age! The divine accommodation is not a sanctioning of the realities of this fallen aeon, but serves as a continual reminder that *what is* ought not to be. God's grace must ever be seen against the background of the divine *no*.

We've ascertained that the commands of Jesus were given in absolute, unconditional form, but those who respond to His call in this age must make their own adjustments in light of their earthly limitations and failures. Martin Dibelius concluded his important study by saying that Jesus proclaims the pure will of God in an absolute way. His will is not confined to an interim and thus is not valid only for a particular period until the end of the world. It is God's actual demand upon men at all times and for all time. But it will attain its full validity only in the Kingdom of God. That the fulfilment of God's will is hampered and embarrassed by the conditions of our worldly existence is the sign of this passing age. In the face of the coming end, Jesus proclaims God's demand without regard to such considerations. His will does not depend upon the Kingdom expectation; it is eternal like Himself. The Kingdom expectation, however, gives the occasion for the proclamation of the divine will, without regard to the circumstances of everyday existence. It makes men free to understand something of the pure, unconditional will of God. Although we are unable to more than partially fulfill it, we can be transformed and guided by it. We are enabled to live more fully in accordance with God's higher intentions, accepting at the same time our responsibility for failures, compromises, and partial fulfillments. And this we can do without fear of losing favor or status with God, because His grace meets us in forgiveness and renewal.

Under the circumstances of this fallen aeon, the *hardness of heart* continues to be a reality which not all Christian couples seem able to escape. The union of man and woman which was designed to be a mutual blessing, can in some instances become such a burden and curse that a continuation of the marriage is the greater of two evils. At this juncture we encounter the divine condescension of grace. We are relieved of the burden of our weakness and failure through the assurance of God's gracious accommodation. He meets us with forgiveness, and with it renewed possibilities for restoration to life at its best. Divine grace in this age precludes all possibility of legalistic penalties prevailing, for we are not under law! Failure reminds man that he is under grace, living constantly within God's forgiveness. Kingdom demands remain as the ideal toward which he orients his life in the Spirit.

It should be perfectly evident by now that we cannot refuse to apply the demands of the Sermon on the Mount to ourselves in all their rigor, all the while recognizing that they are not meant for us to be a new law, but an ethical ideal. The sanctions and penalties give way to grace. The Sermon on the Mount serves as a constant protest against the present fallen age, and keeps us from losing sight of the provisional character of this age. Life now involves contradiction, conflict, and compromise. Our choices are sometimes limited to the lesser of two evils. Principles often stand in tension with each other. The absolute, radical demands of the Sermon on the Mount do not fit this age perfectly. For Christians they become a guide to the true righteousness, not just unfulfillable law. Through such examples of Kingdom righteousness and law we are challenged to the very highest which the Holy Spirit might accomplish in and through us. In this way we should be signs of the coming Kingdom, signs that something has already begun. In our lives the reign of God should be visible, showing forth something of the powers of the age to come.

Some will fail in the area of marital relationship. In His radicalizing of the Mosaic Law, Jesus could not call hate *murder*, or lust *adultery*, without also calling divorce and remarriage *adultery* as well. This is the ultimate judgment of God's pure will for marriage. In this age, as we have seen, it is conditioned by His forgiving grace. The Kingdom message in the Synoptics must be received in light of the changed conditions under grace as expressed in the Epistles. Whenever this is the case, when a marital failure which in the ultimate process of things renders divorce inevitable—the lesser of two evils—then remarriage may well be God's gracious will. The whole tenor of the New Testament Epistles would support such a view. This is what the great John Milton called, "God's gracious indulgence . . . the good work of parting those whom nothing holds together."

8

As Jesus Declared It to Be

Our attention now turns directly to the words of Jesus as recorded in Matthew 19:3–9. Of the four places where Jesus' word on divorce and remarriage is to be found, two have special significance, and both are in Matthew's Gospel. The first is in the special context of Matthew 5:31, 32—the Sermon on the Mount. An entire chapter has been devoted to this special context. Now our chief attention focuses upon Matthew 19:3–9. In scholarly consideration, this passage often is regarded as the highest development of Jesus' sayings, containing the greatest number of components to be found in any of the accounts. This has attracted scholars to try to trace a development from a primitive to a more advanced statement. The Roman Catholic scholar, Dominic Crossan, provides one of the best summaries of a five-stage development. Briefly, we shall consider, then criticize this view. Since this form of approach has gained some measure of popularity, it will be well to see that it could be assimilated into the major thesis of this book, but is really unnecessary and an unacceptable alternative to the view upon which this book is built. The literary development of the four texts consists of two parts: First, the development of an isolated saying, which in this writer's opinion represents the will of God, unconditioned by man's sinfulness and failure, ever standing as the ethical ideal. This is expressed in Luke 16:18 without any context, for it needs none. It is the pure intention of God in the Creation orders. No problem situation calling for a possible exception is under consideration. In the mind of the Spirit of God who is the Author of the Gospels, such problem situations and possible exceptions under the law shall be taken up elsewhere and in due time. As to the development of this isolated saying, it can only be said that the time and place of this setting are now lost to us.

Next, the saying is integrated into the development of another setting, that of a debate with the Jewish authorities. We shall note briefly the five stages in the process of development.

Matthew 5:31, 32 represents the earliest statement of the saying, although in a later setting and in a very special context of ethical absolutes from the lips of the King. In this early statement there is no explicit question of monogamy. Among the Jews, adultery was an act against the right of the husband only. This text is against divorce and remarriage on the woman's part. It says nothing of the former husband. This, then, could be regarded as the most primitive form of the saying, looking only to what the husband should not do to his wife in the context of Mosaic Law.

The second stage in the development is represented by the completely isolated statement in Luke 16:18. The point of view is still primarily that of the husband, but monogamy is also presumed. Adultery is committed when the husband divorces the wife and he marries another; the second husband of the divorced wife is also in adultery. What is new in this saying is that the former husband is also said to commit adultery in remarrying—it is committed against the rights of the former wife. This is a definite advance in concept. The isolated statement of Luke 16:18 is embedded as it is into Matthew 19:3–9 in what we shall see is a higher level of transmission. It is clear that monogamy is being presumed at the same time that divorce and remarriage for either party is being prohibited.

Mark 10:11, 12 marks the third stage of development. Here attention is equally divided between husband and wife for the first time; the passage is structurally paralleled between the two. The viewpoint is no longer exclusively male as in Matthew 5, or even primarily male as in Luke 16 and its parallel in Matthew 19. Rather, it is completely balanced between both husband and wife. If the husband divorces his wife and remarries, he commits adultery (v. 11); if the wife divorces her husband and remarries, she commits adultery (v. 12). No mention is made of the new partners of either.

Fourth, Mark 10:11, 12 is made an appendage to Mark 10:2–9.

The fifth and final stage is the transition of Mark 10:2–9 into Matthew 19:3–9, with the complete integration of the saying into the now newly phrased debate.

Now, although we do not generally consider this reconstruction valid, we do know that Matthew, like Luke, is dependent upon sources, among which we identify the more primitive Gospel of Mark. Nearly all of Mark is gathered up in Matthew or in Luke, with much of his Gospel in both. Matthew 19 is on all accounts the most pivotal passage of the four, distinctive in that it alone contains the combination of two clauses, namely, the exceptive clause and the remarriage clause. Each of these appear elsewhere, as we have noted, but only in Matthew 19:3–9 are they coordinated. So it is with variously supported reasons that we concentrate our attention upon this single Gospel passage in an attempt to grasp all that Jesus taught on divorce and remarriage, noting at the same time that this teaching is guided and limited by its specific context. With assurance, we can only say that we understand the mind of Jesus insofar as He speaks to the particular context and the specific questions addressed to Him. To generalize beyond that we are unwilling to do, for this is the very procedure on the part of many scholars with which we take most serious exception.

The passage begins in Matthew 19 by setting the scene; it is a debate scene: "And Pharisees came up to him and tested him

by asking, 'Is it lawful to divorce one's wife for any cause?' "
(v. 3).

Let us be careful to notice the limits of the situation: Jesus is
faced by the Pharisees—Jewish authorities—who come to test
Him. It is not as though Jesus gathered His disciples and said,
"Now I'm going to teach you about divorce and remarriage—
how it has been under Mosaic Law, how it will be under the
Kingdom reign, and how it will be during the interim Church
period of grace." No. He is tested by Jewish authorities.

Our second consideration is the nature of the test, "Is it lawful to divorce one's wife for any cause?" What do they mean by
lawful? They mean one thing: What does the law of Moses
allow? Now, categorically, it would be incorrect to dissociate
this passage from the category of instances where Jesus and the
Jewish authorities disputed about points of Jewish law. Here we
note particularly the distinctive place which the word *lawful* has
in Matthew. Four times Matthew tells us how Jesus is challenged as to what is lawful. In each instance it is the Pharisees
who challenge Him, and the question is always His relation to
the law, whether it be His teaching or His conduct. "Is it lawful
to [give tribute] to Caesar . . . ?" (22:17) or again, "Is it lawful
to heal on the sabbath?" (12:10). And it is no different in
Matthew 19. It should be apparent that these are similar situations. The demand upon Jesus is equally clear: He is bound to
answer them in strict accordance with their question, giving
neither less than they ask, nor more. As Guy Duty puts it, "The
Pharisees had Jesus' answer to *their* question, as presented by
them—and as understood by them." This is quite a different
question than Christians are asking today! And Jesus didn't address Himself to any such questions as we would ask today, for
this was outside of the situation. But interestingly enough, when
later He was questioned further by His disciples (vv. 10–12), He
did not go into the matter any deeper. He stayed within the ethical context of the law even then.

Clearly, the scene is an attempt to discredit Jesus before the
law, and at the same time involve Him in a burning controversy
of the day. In the evil logic of His detractors, whatever side
Jesus takes, He will lose. Elsewhere we have described the two
rabbinic schools which flourished in the century before Jesus
came, the schools of Shammai and Hillel. Recall the conservative character of Shammai, the liberal tendencies of Hillel. In
the question of divorce, Shammai held that only sexual immorality was a valid cause, whereas Hillel included the broadest spec-
trum of causes, including so trivial a matter as the wife forget-
ting to salt her husband's food. Understandably, the school of
Hillel was the most popular by far! And now the Pharisees sense
that if Jesus sides with Hillel he will show Himself to be a traitor
to the law as *some* would interpret the law. If He sides with
Shammai, He will lose His popularity with the majority. They
fully expect to catch Jesus on the horns of dilemma. Our Lord's
mastery of every situation is nowhere more in evidence than in
this situation.

> He answered, "Have you not read that he who made them from
> the beginning made them male and female, and said, 'For this
> reason a man shall leave his father and mother and be joined to
> his wife, and the two shall become one'? So they are no longer
> two but one. What therefore God has joined together, let no man
> put asunder.
>
> Matthew 19:4–6

Jesus points beyond the law of Moses to the order of Creation, and in doing so does not directly answer their question. He
points to the divine institution of marriage, and in tacitly ac-
knowledging the right of divorce and remarriage under the Mosaic
Law, Jesus is saying that this was not the case in the beginning.
The original purpose of God, never abrogated, was that the marriage union should remain indissoluble. That ideal has not
changed. He calls them back to the fact that a married couple
are intrinsically one; their unity is established in the purpose of

God. All else has been forsaken to form this union. Then Jesus adds, "What therefore God has joined together, let no man put asunder." Taken in itself, this saying of Jesus may not be used to prove that divine law forbids any and all divorce; that is reading into it more than it says. Jesus here is speaking of God's original purpose in instituting marriage. It is not individual marriages that Jesus primarily has in mind; it is God's joining of husbands and wives that is meant by, "What God has joined together" (not *Whom*). For men to deliberately cause the breakdown of marriage—as was then being done by these followers of Hillel especially—is to frustrate the purpose of God in instituting marriage. Note that Jesus does not take opportunity to distinguish between what He would consider true marriages and those unions not in accordance with God's will; He is unconcerned to define: "What God has joined together." He simply draws the corollary of God's intention, namely, that what God has instituted, no one should destroy. Here is a warning to anyone who brings a marriage to an end or encourages it. This, however, does not necessarily conflict with the reality of any given marriage which because of its own internal breakdown has come to an end already.

Not having been given an answer to their question, the Pharisees then said, "Why then did Moses command one to give a certificate of divorce, and to put her away?" He said to them, "For your hardness of heart Moses allowed you to divorce your wives, but from the beginning it was not so" (vv. 7, 8). Jesus has now joined the issue squarely and declared Himself. Worth noticing, too, is a reversal of terms. In Matthew 19:7 the Pharisees' question was couched in the words, "Why then did Moses command . . . ." Jesus was careful in His reply to say, "Moses allowed . . . ." He corrected it from *command* to *allowed*. But in Mark 10 it is reversed. The Pharisees said, "Moses allowed . . ." (v. 4) and Jesus replied that he *commanded* (v. 5). But wait—in Mark the question has to do with the bill of divorcement. Whereas, in Mark, Jesus recognized divorce as a social reality that required regulation, in Matthew, Jesus was simply careful not to let it seem that divorce was commanded by Moses, only permitted as a concession to human failure.

Jesus' phrase, *for your hardness of heart,* means "out of regard to your hardness of heart," which John Murray thinks means the stubbornness of the Israelites, a situation of moral perversity and obliquity arising from their insubordination to and rebellion against the will of God. But, really, is this not just placing the harshest possible construction upon the words? It would appear a less danger of extremism to take the words more nearly for what they say. *Hardness of heart* may mean no more than that married couples face insoluble conflict and lack of ability to bring their separate lives together in an organic whole, in consequence of which there is frustration, anger, and entrenched pessimism. Spirits that have become dulled and hardened in this condition could easily be referred to as having hardness of heart. This would be most commonly the case in marital disappointment and breakup. This would more naturally speak to marital difficulties as we know them in our time. Romans 7 and Galatians 5 make it evident that hardness of heart is a continuing problem in human relationships, yes, even at times in Christian relationships. The question arises: *But does not Redemptive Realism place man under God's conditional will in our time—the time of grace—even as was the case under the Mosaic Law?* This surely would be our supposition from reading the New Testament Epistles. What then shall Jesus say and what does He mean? For whose exact benefit is He saying what He says?

A principle developed in this study is that there are different ethical administrations of God's will, one of which represents His unconditional will, three of which represent His conditional will. During man's innocence he was governed by God's unconditional will; this is what Jesus meant by the words, ". . . but from the beginning it was not so" (v. 8). He Himself gave tacit recognition to the different ethical context which came into existence with man's fall, and in time the law of Moses as its first governing law. Not only that, but Jesus proceeded directly to the pronouncement of His own "law." He said without any qualification, "And I say to you: whoever divorces his wife, except for unchastity, and marries another, commits adultery" (v. 9). Yet perhaps Jesus was not laying down a new law as much as He was simply revealing the reality of marriage. And furthermore, He did not say—although He certainly might have had He wished—"It was not so from the beginning, and shall not be so among any who follow Me." If anything is worthy of notice, it is that Jesus did not at all deny the place of divorce in the fallen world of which His people are a part. He did not restore "from the beginning" as though He were teaching, "As it was in the beginning, so shall it be from now on."

It should not be necessary to comment on the question of whether Jesus was talking about divorce or only separation. But some seek to make this distinction in order to avoid the clear meaning of divorce as dissolution. In all Jewish history, divorce was called "a cutting off." The Mosaic divorce bill was called by the Jews "A Bill of Cutting Off." There was never any question but what Judaism meant complete dissolution. Now, the Greek word *apoluo* is the exact equivalent of the Old Testament *kerithuth,* and has the same precise meaning of absolute dissolution. One is reminded of Dean Henry Alford's comment that we must not violate the known usage of a word and substitute another for which there is no precedent. Every precedent in the Bible meant dissolution. So, when our Lord spoke about divorce, He must have had in mind the complete severance of the marriage bond. That was the only meaning His hearers could possibly attach to the word. We conclude that the first-century New Testament reader would understand "put away" to mean absolute dissolution with the right of remarriage.

At this point we confront the exceptive clause found only in the text of Matthew. The Revised Standard Version reads, "except for unchastity." In the King James Version the word is translated "fornication." Fornication and adultery are terms used interchangeably in the New Testament. It is thus that the English word *unchastity* is more commonly employed today. It refers to illicit sexual intercourse in general. The word *fornication* was widely used for *adultery,* and this usage had been well established in Greece for several centuries prior to the coming of Christ. As for the Jews, fornication commonly referred to incest, sodomy, bestiality, and all forms of forbidden sex acts (*see* Leviticus 20:11–21). Thus Jesus entered the debate only to give His own judgment; He did not take sides with either school of thought—Shammai or Hillel. He was equally ambiguous in saying it was "for your hardness of heart." But as to actual causes, He did not speak. What He did say was that His own superseding interpretation of the law of Moses directs that only unchastity is a valid cause. Greek scholarship understands *except for* to signify an exclusion—an exceptional cause for which an action is rightly taken. Unchastity is that single, rightly taken exception because by nature it accomplishes the real dissolution of the marriage bond in what is to be regarded certainly as one of the basic bonding aspects of marriage—sexual intercourse. Certainly, unchastity breaks that which is fundamentally constitutive of marriage.

It is to be anticipated that this cause—unchastity—will not be regarded as the all-embracing cause for marriage dissolution by many moderns. With this we are inclined to agree. For it is not sexual intercourse alone that constitutes a marriage. William Barclay notes: "Marriage is given, not that two people should do one thing together, but that they should do all things together." We, too, would say that, along with sexual intercourse as constitutive of marriage, there must be consent and commitment. Thus the death of marriage may very well be internal, not external. When consent and commitment are detracted for whatever reason—in all likelihood because love is lost and there remains no emotional bond—marriage for all real purposes dies. Or a marriage may continue to maintain itself as a sexual relationship but be a marriage in name only. We can argue—with mature understanding—that the union of bodies sexually is essential and constitutive if, and only if, it presupposes a union of mind and heart in persons committed to each other completely. Sexual acts, which are most intimate, hardly constitute marriage where the common life and union of mind and heart are absent. It is the intimate life and love of two persons that leads to their natural expression in sexual union, but not the converse. The physical acts of marriage, in other words, are not marriage itself. Marriage implies bodily acts, but it is not merely a contract for such bodily acts. Marriage is a commitment leading to a total way of life, a shared partnership of all of life. Marriage is more than the legal consent to a contract for physical activity. Why then did Jesus make unchastity—the physical side of marriage only—the single consideration around which divorce could be validated? If our task was to adapt the biblical revelation to our present understanding of the psychology of interpersonal relations, the problem admittedly would be difficult. Instead, ours is to recognize that God who speaks is God who has created mankind, and that His purpose is our ultimate consideration. All through Scripture runs the theme of sexual exclusivity as the constitutive sign of the marital union. Not only is it constitutive, but it is symbolic of the total union of persons—mind, spirit, and body. So intimate is the sexual union when it is fused with love and commitment, that it is the unique carrier of emotional and spiritual meanings of marriage. It symbolizes as nothing else can the exclusive commitment of two people to each other. The biblical perspective is that marriage needs sex and sex needs marriage, and both need to be fused in the bonds of man's spirit. God has appointed sexual intercourse within marriage to be the sign and symbol of intimate union. It is, after all, God's prerogative to appoint what He will, and this He has appointed.

It may be that some readers are puzzled by the fact that the

exceptive clause is found in Matthew, but not in the other two
Synoptic Gospels. We have noted one method of dealing with
this problem, namely to see the passages that do not contain the
exception—Mark and Luke—as an earlier form of the saying
which underwent an alteration in the later light of the Church's
experience. This we considered untenable. Another approach is
equally unacceptable, although it is held by some evangelicals.
This is the suggestion that the exception does not come from the
lips of Jesus, but is an editorial insertion of Matthew's to conform Jesus' words to the statements found in the Old Testament.
Matthew, in other words, deduced this exception from a sense
of Jesus' conformity with the Old Testament, and simply added
it to the recorded words of Jesus. It may serve as a solution to
the problem, but it is not a satisfactory solution. It renders the
account of Matthew unreliable, and is an unnecessary tampering
with the record. R. V. G. Tasker comments: "Nor is it defensi-
ble, on scholarly considerations, to justify a rigorous attitude to
divorce by ruling out the words *except it be for fornication* as an
interpolation on the ground that they are not found in the parallel passage in Mark." As we shall see, it is not necessary to
choose between the two readings and to reject the exceptive
clause or else put it in the mouth of Matthew instead of Jesus.
Let us give the matter some further consideration.

The exceptive clause recorded in both Matthean passages
qualifies the other two texts in Mark and Luke. The question
arises whether Matthew records Jesus' words with their original
qualification while Mark and Luke omitted this qualification, or
whether Mark and Luke record the unqualified absolutes of
Jesus, and Matthew has taken it upon himself to append the
qualifying exception. Modern scholarship tends toward the position that it is Matthew's addition, not the omission of Mark and
Luke. Reasons given are as follows: First, Paul would then have
to represent a third omission of the exceptive clause in 1 Corinthians 7, giving three omissions in all. Three writers would have

then omitted the clause, each doing so separately. No reasons for this seem available. Second, the addition of qualifying clauses to make the statements of Jesus more precise for Matthew's particular audience is regarded by some as a well-founded characteristic of Matthew, hence quite acceptable here. Finally, we can hardly argue against the exceptive clause as not being supported by manuscript tradition.

Now, this is enough for such conjectures. It is not necessary to ask whether Jesus gave only the absolute, unexceptional statement of Mark and Luke. It is not as though the two stand in contradiction and require any such explanations as those given above. This is conceding too much. Perhaps the more relevant question is why Jesus may have given the saying as an absolute prohibition in one instance, yet supply an exceptive clause in another? We have already given one possibility: He may well have declared the absolute, pure intention of God in confirmation of the orders of Creation. This would unequivocally declare His affirmation of the original intent of God. Then, in the face of the realities of the fallen world, and in harmony with the Old Testament provision, He made a practical accommodation. Inasmuch as we believe the Holy Spirit is the One who supervises the formulating of the scriptural material, we can believe that it was His mind to include both statements for these very purposes. It has been a deeply considered part of this study to trace the declarations of both God's unconditional will and those of His conditional will. It seems not too much to allow the same distinction to govern our acceptance of both absolute and qualified statements of Jesus. While the absolute statement fits the order of Creation, the exception fits the human condition to which God makes His accommodation in grace. May we not expect to find assertions of an absolute kind which correspond to our understanding of God as absolute? And may we not also expect to find those absolutes set aside whenever they prohibit the extension of God's mercy and grace?

Another concern of some scholars is whether the exception applies only to the divorce clause or to both the divorce-and-remarriage clause. The present writer is convinced that the exception applies to both divorce and remarriage. A. T. Robertson remarks that in the Greek sentence, as in the English, it does not matter which position in the sentence the exception takes. It can be at the beginning, middle, or end, and the meaning of the law remains the same. But the exception sounds better in the middle of the Greek sentence and it is the proper place for it to be. The exception can be removed from its usual position and placed in an unusual position in the sentence without changing its bearing on both clauses. With Robertson and others it is our opinion that both divorce and remarriage are considered together under the exception. Were this not the case, it would seem necessary to clarify the issue inasmuch as the Pharisees were not questioning the right to remarry—this was never questioned on the basis of the Old Testament's clear provision for it.

It is most interesting that Jesus did not take this prime opportunity to declare Shammai's strict interpretation as correct, although tacitly He seems to make this view His own. Surely, He did not hesitate simply because it would have jeopardized His popularity! However close His own view to that of Shammai, Jesus was not in the least concerned with the debate as such. He was the law's sovereign interpreter. He did not merely agree with one school of its interpreters. Jesus remained above any human agreement, and instead He places a completely new construction on the matter: He interprets the Mosaic Law so that divorce where no unchastity is involved is tantamount to adultery. This was most startling, because Moses' bill of divorce placed no conditions upon the divorced person except that he could not remarry the person he divorced. Neither did the Mosaic Law say that remarriage was adultery. Jesus is thus giving a more rigorous interpretation to the law, that which supersedes the Mosaic requirements. In this, Jesus is once again seen taking

His place as the Messiah who has come to announce the Kingdom and its higher ethic.

In what sense can Jesus mean: ". . . whoever divorces his
wife, except for unchastity, and marries another, commits adultery," and the additional saying from Matthew 5:32: ". . . and
whoever marries a divorced woman commits adultery"? Certainly he does not mean actual adultery. It is an extension of the
reality of having violated the ideal, which is intrinsic indissolubility of the marriage bond as far as God's intention is concerned. With Ray Anderson we would say, "This is most certainly true in the absolute ethic of the marriage vow. Adultery in
this sense is not the definition of one's moral life but the
definition of one's ethical relationship to the absoluteness of the
marriage vow. When the party of a previous marriage relationship is still living, the remarriage always involves ethical adultery." He uses the term *ethical adultery* in contrast to actual
adultery, and it reminds us of Jesus' words in the Sermon on the
Mount, "But I say to you that every one who looks at a woman
lustfully has already committed adultery with her in his heart"
(Matthew 5:28). Again, this is not actual adultery, but ethical
adultery—violation of God's ethical intent. Although not the literal action of sin, it is nonetheless plainly a contradiction of
God's absolute ethic, His pure intent, and thus should be confessed as that which requires moral acknowledgment and a peni-
tent heart.

Victor Pospishil provides a useful distinction when he speaks
of the intrinsic indissolubility and extrinsic indissolubility. Intrinsic has to do with the inward ethical meaning of a marriage
union. Extrinsic refers to that which can take place between two
married persons in actuality. The absolute intent of God as expressed in the original state of marriage knew no indissolubility.
Thus we can say that God provided for no intrinsic dissolubility
in marriage. The creative purpose of God equates with absolute
intrinsic indissolubility of any and every marriage. This intrinsic

aspect of God's pure intent can never change. In the actual disablement of human life through sin's work in mankind, it is extrinsic dissolution that is a reality which sometimes is inescapable. Jesus reaffirmed the intrinsic indissolubility of marriage —the unchangeableness of God's intent. Within the framework of the Mosaic Law as elevated by the higher vision of Kingdom Law which will be in effect when Jesus reigns, adultery is recognized as bringing about extrinsic dissolubility, for it breaks the constitutive symbol which God has appointed. To break bodily affiliation, in God's eyes, is to symbolize the personal sundering in an ultimate way. It is recognizable in divorce. If we take the legal reference of Jesus to the Pharisees, and apply it to the ethical context of grace, perhaps Jesus is saying to Christians today, "Marriage intrinsically is always indissoluble, but under the conditions of the Old Aeon, and also under the conditions of Redemptive Realism, marriage extrinsically is dissoluble at times. When the living symbols of the one-flesh union cease to exist, when love and unity of spirit no longer live, then dissolution may become the tragic moral choice, the lesser of two evils. To maintain the relationship merely to preserve the image of faithfulness along with legal unity when the marriage has died may only destroy one or both personalities through indignity and unreality."

Back to Matthew 19:3-9 before this chapter closes—it would appear that Jesus instituted two provisions in contradiction to the Mosaic Law. He abrogated the Mosaic penalty for adultery, which was death, and He legitimated divorce for the cause of unchastity. This is seen by some as the most concrete, conspicuous instance of Jesus' exercise of original legislative authority as the Messianic King. The implication is that jurisprudence respecting divorce in Jesus' Kingdom shall be more stringent than in the Mosaic administration—not characterized by the same laxity in toleration of divorce. How Jesus would actually deal with a concrete situation is not indicated in any of the divorce passages. This is something which would have to be determined from other contexts.

R. V. G. Tasker perceptively comments that Jesus is not laying down in these words addressed to the Pharisees any fixed rule which must be followed by His disciples at all times in the future. It is strange, he says, that Christians—who have been ready enough to see that Jesus is not legislating in dealing with other matters of conduct—have often been reluctant to bring the same consideration to their interpretation of His teaching on marriage and divorce. Tasker says, "No fixed rules therefore about divorce could possibly have been given which were equally capable of being applied to Christians in the first and in the twentieth centuries. The only static factors are, first, that the divine ideal for the relationship of men and women remain the same, and secondly, that men and women remain the same frail creatures who often find it extremely difficult to achieve in a particular marriage relationship the unity which could alone be truthfully described as 'a joining together by God.' Jesus, we may surely believe, expects His followers, far from perfect themselves, to recognize this frailty, and to treat it with sympathy; and it may well be that all who fail to do so have not yet fully learned the lesson of the story of Jesus and the woman taken in adultery found in John viii. 1–11."

Our study of Jesus' teaching on divorce and remarriage has emphasized its placement in the special contexts of the Synoptic Gospels and especially in the Gospel of Matthew. Those contexts are either oriented wholly toward the Mosaic Law of the past or to the Kingdom Law which largely concerns the special conditions of the eschatological Kingdom yet to come. In the divorce passages themselves there is nothing redemptive which Christians can directly associate with the ethical context of grace which dominates the message to the Church in the Epistles. Interestingly, neither Paul nor any other of the apostles reaffirm this legislation in the Epistles. When the same subject

matter is touched upon, it is with a different approach; the legislative aspects are absent. Paul does not address himself to all the
questions which arise in the complex area of marriage, divorce,
and remarriage. He addresses himself only once to this subject,
and that is to special questions sent to him from the church at
Corinth. His answers are confined apparently to the questions
addressed to him. He nowhere attempts to declare a law of divorce and remarriage, nor does he attempt a general teaching on
the subject. To examine just what Paul does say is the task that
lies before us in the next chapter. There we shall be largely concerned with his First Letter to the Corinthians, and especially
chapter seven. Then we shall briefly touch upon the passage in
Romans 7:1–4.

9

Divorce and Remarriage in the Epistles

It is a curious thing that the only major reference to divorce and remarriage to be found anywhere in the Epistles is the seventh chapter in First Corinthians. Curious, because one would suppose that such a basic problem in human life would surely merit fuller discussion and instruction. We cannot doubt that the Author of Scripture foresaw the history of the Church, especially these latter days when so many conditions combine to make marriage a difficult, troubled institution. Paul wrote to the Corinthians in answer to their specific questions and problems. He did not write in answer to *our* specific questions and problems, nor could he, really. But this only creates an additional problem for us today. Legitimately we ask, "Is Paul's word in First Corinthians the last word on the subject?" Let us hope not! We have only to read what Paul said about singlehood to be impressed that he spoke to very special circumstances. To generalize from his comments there would be disastrous. Some of the misfounded criticisms of the ethical attitudes of the Church come from those who isolate such texts from the remainder of the New Testament and point to what may then be considered a very narrow and negative view. But again, the context is everything. And the ethic of a particular situation like that in Corinth must be correlated with other ethical contexts in the New Testament, or we misread it for ourselves. So we face some very special considerations in the study of this chapter.

As we turn from the statements of Jesus in the Synoptic Gospels to the Epistles, one can almost hear some say, "All right, what you have written is all quite convincing to this point. There is no question but that Jesus often is speaking in a context which has to do primarily with the Old Testament law and a correct interpretation of its meaning. Clearly, He radicalizes that law for the higher conditions and demands of the Kingdom Age. He does seem to declare that new law as though the coming of the Kingdom were just then to happen. His sayings are found in an eschatological setting, with the Kingdom perceived as imminent. He also provides strong reminders of God's creative purposes for marriage, purposes that did not envision dissolution of what intrinsically is indissoluble. He continually points to conditions that will prevail when the Old Aeon ceases to be and the King reigns over His Kingdom. The Kingdom Law, with its heightened and narrowed conditions does not become a new law for the Church Age, but serves as an ethical ideal, the principles of which apply to our time although the legal, absolute judgments do not. We are also very conscious that no provision is made for possible failure, no Redemptive Realism breaks through at all. It is not a context of grace, but law. All of this fits into place and is quite convincing, but what about Paul? He speaks directly to the New Testament Church of which we are a part, and doesn't he virtually seem to repeat the words of Jesus? For all practical purposes, doesn't this put us right back into the same ethical conditions we find in the Gospels? Is Paul's teaching really any different?"

In all the New Testament Epistles—the detailed specification of Christian life and conduct—there is but one major passage, strangely enough, that touches on the question of divorce and remarriage. It is in the one Epistle most fully devoted to correcting abuses and answering questions. These are very specific questions that are addressed to Paul, and he gives very specific answers. Most obviously, it is a fundamental feature of this passage that it is not generalized teaching on the subject of marriage, divorce, and remarriage. It simply cannot qualify as that, for it is fragmentary as to subject matter, and exclusively devoted to apparently two questions which the Corinthians raised. For these reasons the chapter cannot form a basic admonition to the Church at large, nor does it anywhere touch upon the destructive marital conditions which spell the death of marriage as sometimes experienced in our time. In fact, nowhere in the Epistles is such teaching to be found. Paul addresses himself to a particular problem which faced a particular church at a particular time. And yet Paul seems to generalize on a number of themes having to do with singleness and marriage.

Chapter 7 opens with the words, found six times in this Epistle: "Now concerning the matters about which you wrote . . ." (1 Corinthians 7:1). The Corinthians had written the Apostle Paul seeking his advice in reference to the state of affairs in their church. One such subject was marriage and divorce. Evidently, from their questioning Paul, there was diversity of opinion in the church. Probably some of Jewish origin thought marriage obligatory, while others thought it undesirable. Paul responds by holding to the biblical roots of marriage as normal and desirable, while at the same time pointing out that in the present circumstances there was reason to regard it as not expedient. So Paul begins his answer by saying, "It is well for a man not to touch a woman. But because of the temptation to immorality, each man should have his own wife, and each woman her own husband" (vv. 1, 2). The phrase *not to touch a woman* is equivalent to "not to marry," and *it is well* means "expedient" here as elsewhere (*see* Matthew 17:4; 18:8, 9; 1 Corinthians 10:23). To strike a balance in the Corinthian divergence of opinion, Paul simply says that there is nothing wrong about not marrying—"It is well." He is not advocating nonmarriage as being superior to marriage. He concedes its acceptability.

In verse 8 Paul says, "To the unmarried and the widows I say

that it is well for them to remain single as I do." Once more Paul
is simply saying that it is well; it is not mandatory that they
marry. There is the tendency to read this as saying that it is
superior to remain single; this Paul does not say. On balance,
Paul simply affirms that singlehood is acceptable. His only
qualification is that should the single person find himself unable
to live with sexual passion, then it is better for him to marry.
Surely, somewhere in the New Testament it is appropriate to
outline the advantages to those who do not marry, lest from
other Scriptures it be assumed that for all persons in all circumstances marriage is mandatory or almost so. Such has never been
the case in all the history of the Church. There are some in
every generation called to singlehood. Never is it ours to repudiate or depreciate this state, despite our persuasion that God
generally calls men and women to the great benefits of marriage.
To give force to this counterposition, Paul teaches against this
specific background of the Corinthian questioning. There it is
relatively easy to understand, and from there other applications
can be made.

To remain single was simply good advice at that particular
time and for those particular Christians. Just why this is the case
is not left to doubt inasmuch as Paul returns to the subject of
singlehood in verses 25 and following. Now he undergirds his
advice with reasons which he had not given previously. In verse
26 he says, "I think then that this is good in view of the present
distress, that it is good for a man to remain as he is" (1 Corinthians 7:26 NAS). Paul's counsel is conditioned by what he calls
"the present distress." Times and conditions are not normal;
the advice which one would normally give is not appropriate for
now. Paul, who could affirm the high view of marriage to the
Ephesians (Ephesians 5:21–32), is not dropping to a low view
here. Rather, he is speaking to a particular time and situation; to
read more into his words does violence to the context.

What was the present distress, and why did it have such

influence upon Paul's counsel to the Corinthians? To understand this is first to deal with a problem of translation. Virtually every English translation in present usage translates the passage as "the present distress" or in similar fashion indicates that it means the stress of the present time. (A curious exception is the Revised Standard Version which reads "the impending distress.") The translations are supported by many commentators as well. As Leon Morris writes, "Little can be said in favor of this meaning the troubles heralding the second advent. Paul's references to Christ's return are not associated with a present distress." William Barclay and a few others notwithstanding, we cannot think Paul was conditioning the marriage institution upon the possible soon return of Christ and the difficulties of the Tribulation to precede it! This tends against the stability of the marriage institution as all of Scripture proclaims it. Many would agree with G. Campbell Morgan's comment: "I think he was referring to local conditions . . . to the pressure of circumstances in the midst of which the church was living at Corinth . . . thinking of Corinth principally." It is most naturally taken as indicating that Paul's friends at Corinth were at that time in unusually difficult circumstances. But does history support this? F. F. Bruce remarks that the movement which Paul inaugurated was attended by tumult and disorder wherever it spread, both in the Roman provinces and in Rome itself. On two occasions, at Philippi and Ephesus, the Book of Acts records the attack of Gentiles on Christian missionaries. On both occasions the reason was a real or imagined threat to vested property interests. Great persecution followed the great fire of A.D. 64, for which the Christians were blamed. At first, Christianity had been regarded as a movement within Judaism and was unharmed by state action. But the earliest persecution, that of Nero in A.D. 64, was the personal crime of one in search of handy scapegoats. Nonetheless, the era of peace was broken; the official policy changed. Twenty years later, in the time of

Domitian, Christianity was recognized as a new force which by its very nature seemed likely to imperil the state. It was forthwith persecuted.

But the distress came not only from the Romans; the Jews sought to destroy the Christian community wherever it could —and there were Jewish centers everywhere in Asia Minor. Conditions in Palestine in the middle years of the first century were marked by years of crisis, and large numbers of people including Christians were already leaving the country. It was the Jerusalem Sanhedrin which prosecuted Jesus before Pilate, and Paul before Felix and Festus; and most of the disturbances which broke out when the gospel was proclaimed in the Roman provinces were fomented by the local Jewish communities, who refused to accept the gospel themselves and were annoyed when their Gentile neighbors believed it. Paul by this time was no stranger to persecution. Read the accounts of his beatings, of his being left for dead at the hands of the Jewish communities of Asia Minor. Corinth at that time was vulnerable. Perhaps even the destruction of Jerusalem and the possibility that this would unleash new waves of Jewish violence against the Christians were within the purview of Paul.

The Greek words literally say: "the distress standing near," and can be translated "present distress" or "impending distress," as the context might indicate. Most likely, Paul was thinking of the present troubles facing the church at Corinth. For Corinth was the commercial capital of Greece, and Canon Farrar tells of the "mass of Jews" in residence, one of the largest colonies of Hellenistic Jews to be found anywhere. In every part of the Empire the hostility of Hellenistic Jews was feared. Although the Proconsul Gallio had dismissed their charges recently (*see* Acts 18) the situation was explosive. Paul's advice to the local Christian community at Corinth was full of solicitude and expediency because of these uneasy times.

Paul uses a strong expression and we do not know all that he had in mind. He might well have been thinking that in the terrible persecutions which were to come, Christians might be put under severe pressures to foreswear Christ in order to save their wives and children from brutal torture and death. Paul was compassionate and practical; he would save his friends from any distress possible if he could. It was indeed anything but normal times, and it called for anything but normal counsel. It is not difficult to read the whole chapter in this light—in fact, one must!

While we shall come to it a little further on, the question of Paul's counsel to the wife who has divorced her husband may also be seen in the light of the peculiarly difficult circumstances of the present time in Corinth. When Paul tells her to remain single or to be reconciled to her husband, may he not perhaps be exercising the same perspective? He would save her from marital entanglements that would prove extremely difficult in the days ahead. This is not altogether improbable.

Can we not see that Paul, contrary to his teaching of the benefits and desirability of marriage elsewhere, says in effect, "Considering your peculiar circumstances at present, it is not expedient for you to marry at this time." This does not contradict the teaching that marriage is honorable (Hebrews 13:4), or that it symbolizes the relation between Christ and His Church (Ephesians 5:31, 32), and as a general rule is necessary to the full development of the individual and the well-being of society. With considerable care, Paul does not take sides with the extreme Jewish party that regarded marriage as obligatory. He simply admits the expediency of all who remain single in times of great difficulty—those, that is, to whom God had given the requisite grace—"But each has his own special gift from God . . ." (v. 7).

This principle of expediency in view of the times is extended to the married in verse 27: "Are you bound to a wife? Do not seek to be free . . ." Here is a tacit admission that it was possible for these Christian spouses to choose to be free. But Paul says this is not fitting, and is to be resisted. This is more in the nature of counsel, not an imperative or command. No impossibility is enjoined; this is not an absolute context of law. Rather, there is the wise word of admonition as to what is presently appropriate or expedient. Easy divorce as it was practiced in those days was to be countered as fully as possible. But it was not absolutely denied.

Notice that Paul does not introduce specific marital problems that even then may have been of magnitude; he simply generalizes that it is not the appropriate thing to desire to be free and to undertake an easy divorce toward that end. It is difficult to see how one can read more into the passage than this. For by the same reasoning (*the present distress*), he continues in verse 27: "Are you free from a wife? Do not seek marriage." What are we to make of this? Shall we assume this to be a command? Or is this wise counsel for the time? Obviously it fits in the same category as the words that preceded, having to do with not seeking to be free from a wife. If taken together, it becomes clear that Paul is quite taken up with the difficult times just ahead of the Church, and he targets in on that. How impressively this comes out in verse 29: "I mean, brethren, the appointed time has grown very short . . . ." Or verse 32: "I want you to be free from anxieties . . . ." Or verse 35: "I say this for your benefit, not to lay any restraint upon you . . . ." William Barclay's comment is that Paul was convinced that he was giving advice for a purely temporary situation. If he had thought otherwise, he would never have written as he did.

This is indeed an enigmatic chapter unless one keeps in mind the background of present distress which governs the whole of Paul's advice. All the more is it significant, in light of the peculiar circumstances which prompted Paul to give counsel which was not related to normal conditions, that these are the only Pauline admonitions touching on divorce and remarriage in all his writings! The Spirit of God did not impel Paul, Peter, James, or John to include any general counsel in their Epistles with reference to divorce and remarriage, nor at any point to reiterate the straight word of Jesus on the subject. How do we account for this? There are two possibilities. The traditional way is simply to conclude that Jesus was so clear and decisive that nothing further need be said—that was the end of the matter. But this is difficult to maintain in light of our studies of the special contexts in which Jesus taught. The other view—which this book maintains—is that this relationship in life is precisely like any other that is subject to failure; whatever falls short of the ethical ideal is subject to redemptive grace which holds the good of the individuals as its end. The Church Age is not under law, but under grace. It is not subject to absolute commands with legally determined consequences. The ultimate consideration is realized forgiveness, renewing grace, restoration to life's highest possibilities. This is no less true of marriage failure than of any other failure.

We come at last to the verses crucial to our study. Our advantage now, however, is that we should be able to view these verses in the larger context of Paul's counsel and to understand the situation which helped to shape his counsel. We are better prepared to receive his words as advice to those who were in very special circumstances, and not to read more into them than that. There is perhaps no greater temptation to the Bible student than to generalize from specific situations, and to give every word in the New Testament a universal application it was never intended to bear.

> To the married I give charge, not I but the Lord, that the wife should not separate from her husband (but if she does, let her remain single or else be reconciled to her husband)—and that the husband should not divorce his wife.
>
> 1 Corinthians 7:10, 11

First, notice that Paul is speaking to these Corinthians in all earnestness, "I give charge . . . ." Second, "not I but the Lord," indicates that Paul's counsel is based on words of the

Lord Himself. To go back to Jesus' words is to find the point of agreement: God's own people are not to divorce; this is something which, as a basic principle, they should not do; it is not God's intention. Yet, how different is the tone and form of Paul's counsel! It is not "cannot" as though an absolute law were being imposed upon all couples in all circumstances. No, the principle of marriage without divorce is reinforced. Actually, Paul does not include what Jesus said, when he charges that the husband should not divorce his wife, for he could have added, "except for unchastity." Why doesn't Paul say all that Jesus said? Because Paul is simply setting forth the general rule—here he is not going into all the special problems which may indeed call for exceptions. He makes no reference to special problems and their redemptive solutions. He is content simply to lay down the Christian ideal. This is what God intends and purposes; this is what the Christian aims for without leaving any doors open. Paul here is unconcerned with engaging in any other considerations that might involve the death of marriage and its necessary consequences. It is as though this matter comes fully within the sphere of historical necessity and the adaptation of spiritual principles to individual situations.

   Verse 10 reads, "To the married I give charge, not I but the Lord, that the wife should not separate from her husband." The word *separate* signifies divorce according to Arndt and Gingrich and other standard Greek lexicons. The scriptural divorce *separated* in the sense that it *divided* the couple and dissolved the union. The Greeks did not recognize divorce as a separation that left the marriage undissolved. Paul would have had to correct their understanding had he meant something other than divorce. For after the age of Homer—when divorce was almost unknown—Attic law allowed the husband to divorce his wife on any cause. The wife could also demand divorce by applying to the Archon and stating her reasons. As in the Jewish world, so in the Greek world of this time—divorce was common. Paul's strong generalizing about divorce and remarriage may well have been his response to the custom of that day—a most necessary response at that. Whether God intends that Paul's counsel be universalized to all Christians in all periods of history is something biblical scholars have the responsibility to weigh.

In verse 11 we have a parenthetic word: "But if she does, let her remain single or else be reconciled to her husband . . . ." Paul gives practical recognition to the unlikely possibility that the absolute ideal will always be obeyed. His acceptance of the relative does not, however, cancel out the absolute. The implication is that a Corinthian wife, under the civil law, could choose to divorce and remarry. Paul admonishes her not to do so. She is urged to remain single or to be reconciled to her husband. Here again is another departure from the teaching of Jesus, for He did not make this recommendation. Why not? Is it because He was talking about divorce on the grounds of unchastity, and could not advise the return to the adulterous partner? Would the Lord have commanded the woman in the case of verse 11 to be reconciled to her husband if she had divorced him for adultery? Surely, Jesus would not give a woman the right to put away an adulterous husband and then command her to be reconciled to him.

Also in verse 11 the Lord is said to be Paul's authority for commanding, "Let not the husband put away his wife" (*see* King James Version). But, again, the Lord had made an exception—a husband could put away his wife for the cause of unchastity. So, now, if the husband is not allowed that exception, he is bound to be "one flesh" with an adulteress! That could hardly be. On the other hand, is Paul talking about divorce on grounds other than unchastity? Does he then hope for reconciliation because there is less reason to divorce? He most certainly must be referring to situations where there was both ground and hope for reconciliation. He cannot be referring to situations where hope is ended. And there are not many today

who deny that there are situations where hope is indeed ended. These are difficult questions, and if nothing else they caution us not to look for a full set of answers to divorce and remarriage in this passage of Scripture.

However we look at this specific problem in the Corinthian church, and the answers Paul gave to their specific questions, we can at least perceive that Paul did not just quote the words of Jesus and indicate that they settled everything. He might have, had that been the solution. His language sounds more like an appeal than a command. He was advising a particular group in a particular situation. We noted earlier how the whole chapter is reflective of Paul's awareness of "the present distress." It is not at all improbable that his advice was a rather strict application of the Lord's absolute statement in view of the prevailing conditions. This is only a conjecture, but it is not groundless. Again, the very complexity of factors surrounding this passage should keep us from sheer dogmatism.

Paul, at any rate, seems to have a nonlegalistic attitude, a noncommanding word of counsel, and he is not reluctant to depart somewhat from the literal word of Jesus as we know it in Matthew's record. That Paul exercises some freedom of interpretation is even clearer in the verses which follow, concerning the Christian with a non-Christian spouse. Without any direct word from the Lord—Paul concedes this in verse 12—he goes beyond the exception which Jesus allowed, and teaches an exception of his own. What we can say for sure is that Paul does not refer to any other specific causes which we know can bring about the death of marriage. He is also generalizing in a specific church situation that sorely needed a strong reinforcing ethical ideal.

It is a most arresting observation that Paul does not simply repeat the unambiguous words of Jesus. Totally foreign to Paul's approach is any radicalized absolute imperative. Neither does Paul find it sufficient to quote Jesus as though this in itself would adequately answer the Corinthians' questions; more is required than that, and that means speaking specifically to a specific question, and tailoring his answer to their particular situation. Since Paul does not even refer to divorce on the ground of unchastity, one can assume the Corinthians didn't ask about such a case, but simply asked about Christians in general divorcing as a customary thing to do. Their one specific question apparently was the one about Christians married to non-Christians. It is here that Paul gets into the scale of values, concerning himself with those instances where the solution seems to lie in a tragic moral choice which weighs the greater against the lesser evil involved. So now we must go on to consider this passage on its own merits.

> To the rest I say, not the Lord, that if any brother has a wife who is an unbeliever, and she consents to live with him, he should not divorce her. If any woman has a husband who is an unbeliever, and he consents to live with her, she should not divorce him . . . . But if the unbelieving partner desires to separate, let it be so; in such a case the brother or sister is not bound. For God has called us to peace. Wife, how do you know whether you will save your husband? Husband, how do you know whether you will save your wife? Only, let every one lead the life which the Lord has assigned to him, and in which God has called him . . . .

1 Corinthians 7:12, 13, 15–17

The Apostle Paul first admits that what follows is not a direct word from the Lord. In fact, what he probably says is that he knows of no ruling of Jesus covering the situation to which he now speaks. This is a new question for Christians of his day: how should they judge the dissolution of pagan-Christian marriages? Paul accepts the historical situation in which the Christian is put by the decision of his non-Christian partner. More than just a concession, it presupposes a theological understanding of the individual situation. God, in His redemptive work, accepts this situation, announcing His gift of freedom, His call to peace, His restoration to new life possibilities. What he warns the Church about is taking the initiative of divorce for the mere reason that the partner is a pagan; this is not a justifiable reason in itself. But this is all that Paul says. Again, he does not get into the question of marriage with a pagan that is complicated by unchastity or any other impossible problem. He is simply addressing himself to the general question of whether a Christian should divorce a pagan partner because that partner is a pagan. The answer clearly is *no*.

Having laid down the general rule, the apostle proceeds to the more urgent and specific question of the pagan partner who wants out of the marriage. When Corinthians became Christians they sometimes faced the displeasure of their spouses, particularly pagan husbands, and sometimes this eventuated in the unbelieving partner divorcing the Christian mate. In view of the Lord's words about divorce, this was cause for anxiety. Was it valid? And here Paul offers them reassurance that cannot possibly set very well today with a multitude of evangelical pastors in the land! Paul says that in such instances the Christian is not to fight it, not to try everything possible to keep the marriage together. Paul is a bit more realistic than many pastors in this regard. He elevates personal peace above the retention of the mere formality of marriage. He recognizes the internal death of marriage as a very real possibility, and especially the nonexistence of a spiritual marriage as certainly a detriment to the Christian spouse, especially if the unbeliever wants out. Paul doesn't try to argue that this is an impossible situation on the biblical grounds of "one flesh," any more than he intimates that the Christian spouse will be an adulteress or adulterer if she or he remarries. This most certainly would have entered the minds of the Corinthians on the basis of what they knew of Jesus' teaching. But Paul does not allow that possibility. Nor does he intimate that the Christian partner should remain unmarried in the hope that the non-Christian mate may at some future time become a Christian and want to return to the marriage. And it is equally clear that the believer is not to keep the door open for the unbeliever to return at any time from the sex orgies of vice-ridden Corinth, to resume the "one flesh" relation with the believer! No! The marriage was dissolved—both by civil law and New Testament consent. The believer was no longer a slave to the marriage. For this is exactly what the word means. The word translated *bondage,* or in our passage, *is not bound,* means "to make a slave of" or "held by constraint of law or necessity." It was a legal term, and whether used with reference to the releasing of a slave, or the divorce of married persons, the meaning clearly was that the persons were no longer held by the constraint of law to the former contract. It meant, for the married person, freedom from all that the marital bond implied. If a slave was legally declared "not under bondage," his former owner had no claim on him whatever. The slave's release was a "bond of relinquishment," or "a contract of renunciation." This is exactly what the bill of divorcement did to the marriage in the case of 1 Corinthians 7:15. The stronger of two verbs that could be used here implies that for the repudiated party to continue bound to the repudiator would be slavery. John Murray and others who have written helpfully on the subject would agree with the summary word of Geoffrey Fisher, "But clearly St. Paul's direction is that a valid marriage may in these circumstances be ended and a new marriage entered into."

Now, let's get to the very heart of Paul's rationale for permitting divorce from an unbeliever who desires it. ". . . For God has called us to peace" (v. 15). What is this but an indirect way of saying that the essence of true marriage is peace, and that a destructively conflicted marriage is sometimes not worth trying to save if one partner is not a Christian. F. W. Grosheide writes, "If, therefore, circumstances are as Paul describes them, the Christian shall resign himself to the divorce. If, due to the conversion of one of the spouses to Christianity, peace has disappeared in a certain marriage, divorce is permissible according to the apostle. This peace is not the same as the absence of domestic quarrels; it is an internal peace granted by God as a blessing upon a good marriage. If this peace would be disturbed by the continuation of a mixed marriage, then the yoke of bondage need not be shouldered but divorce is permissible.''

There is a higher principle than that of merely trying to retain a marriage contract and living together; that higher principle is a relationship of peace. But wait! Jesus never said anything like that! He never intimated at all that a marriage might better be dissolved if peace could not be maintained. Yet Paul undertakes to say just that. The call by God to peace in the marital bond is placed over against the word of Christ forbidding divorce except for unchastity. These differing statements are reconciled when Paul is regarded to be the voice of God to the Church, and Jesus in the Synoptic accounts to be the voice of God to those to whom the Kingdom and its law was an imminent possibility. So Paul is not in any way denying the authority of Jesus as expounded in the Gospels, nor is he in any way superseding that authority. Rather, he is saying that though marriage ought not to be dissolved, there are more important values than that of preserving the semblance of marriage as a formal contract in every instance. Divorce may be allowed when spiritual values are at stake, the peace which marriage is to encompass, in particular. Marriage is made for persons, not persons for marriage, and therefore the person is never to be sacrificed to preserve the marriage. In this sense Paul goes beyond the initial question of whether divorce is to be allowed. This may come as quite a surprise to those who have never thought upon the matter deeply, but it is in full harmony with the New Testament principles of grace. Apparently Paul saw no contradiction of his teaching with Christ's prohibition of divorce and remarriage. He was guided by the Spirit not to mention the exception of unchastity while declaring on his own authority the exception of the unbeliever, and that on the rationale of preserving peace. What does this say to us but that there is *a principle of adaptation* within the New Testament. The indissolubility of marriage is an absolute in God's purpose; marriage is intrinsically indissoluble in terms of God's design. But extrinsically, under the conditions of the Old Aeon, divorce is sometimes seen in the service of Christian peace, indeed sometimes inevitably conditioned by it.

What must be evident to the student of New Testament ethics is that there is a scale of values put before the redeemed community which lives within the continuing limits of human weakness and failure. Indissoluble marriage is a value on that scale; so also is a life of peace. In this world, those two values may be found at times in irresolvable tension. The Pauline exception regards peace as the higher value in such instances. It is only those who look at marriage legalistically who cannot understand this.

One is impressed that, directly following this declaration of freedom, Paul reinforces his counsel, not with a theological word or an ethical word, but with a practical question, "Wife, how do you know whether you will save your husband? Husband, how do you know whether you will save your wife?" In other words, "Don't seek to hold the unbelieving partner; there is no guarantee that in so doing you will be the instrument of his or her salvation." Paul in this instance actually goes so far as to counter the principle laid down in Peter 3:1, 2 to the extent of saying that a Christian cannot forsake peace just because of the hope that the partner will be won to Christ. Marriage is no missionary institution. Bondage and quarreling which are certain need not be accepted in order to achieve a highly uncertain goal. While some seek to read this passage as though it expressed optimism over the possibility of the partner being won to Christ, this seems totally contrary to the structure of the statement. This seems clear enough when the words are seen in their order, ". . . the brother or sister is not bound. For God has called us to peace." The word *for* is the key. And so the sense of the passage is, "Let him go. You are not bound to the marriage. You are rather called to peace, not marital conflict with an unbeliever who wants out. So why remain in bondage when you do not know whether by so doing you can win your partner to Christ!"

Now, what if it were not an unbelieving husband who wanted a divorce, but a carnal, disobedient Christian? Peace is at stake here, too. Might the same exception apply? Apparently Paul wasn't asked such a question. He generalized against divorce, but did not deal with other possible exceptions.

The unique character of Paul's advice is established by the common reference to "the Pauline exception." He does go beyond the word of Jesus as we have it recorded, and this is highly significant in itself. Furthermore, this is not a question of desertion, as so commonly conceived. The pagan partner wants out of the marriage. And for any Hellenistic Jew this would not ever mean merely separation; this was unknown both to Jew and Greek. The pagan partner wanted divorce, not separation, and that is what he got. Paul is not introducing a radical innovation, namely, separation that was less than marital dissolution! If he were, he would have had to explicate it clearly and support it with a rationale. This he did not do. Furthermore, neither Jew nor Greek ever questioned the right to remarry following divorce. Paul does not intimate here that one who remarries is an adulterer. Nor, when Church discipline is set forth in the New Testament, is there even a hint that divorced and remarried Christians are subject to this discipline. Church sanctions against the divorced and remarried are totally foreign to Scripture.

In the writer's judgment, the paragraph cannot close without verse 17, which in the Revised Standard Version is made the beginning of a new paragraph. It seems a more natural transition to close the paragraph we have just studied with verse 17, "Only, let every one lead the life which the Lord has assigned to him, and in which God has called him. This is my rule in all the churches.'' The transitional word is *only*. The principle stated in this verse applies to that which goes before and introduces other applications which follow. When this is made the case, the larger idea which Paul presents might be stated as follows: God has called us to peace above all things else. He has called us to the possibility of living a life unhindered by such destructive conflicts as sometimes occur to destroy the meaning of marriage. This is especially true when one partner is a non-Christian. But the life which God has assigned to us as believers is a life of peace in the body of believers. If one can retain a marriage with an unbeliever and live in peace in the body of believers and with that spouse, good and well. If not, and the partner wants out, this, too, is acceptable. A Christian is not bound to the marital contract in such a situation, but is free to reorder life in its fullest possibilities through another marriage contract. God may be glorified in the new marriage, and a couple may indeed find this their opportunity to fulfill the order of Creation for a truly one-flesh marriage. What was impossible to achieve in the first marriage is fulfilled in the second. Believers have an assigned life in the Body of Christ.

Is this doing violence to the passage? Not so. For Paul later applies the same principle to slaves. They are to remain in their state and not assume that their Christian conversion entitles them to forsake their social station. But this is not the end of it. Paul says in verse 21, ''. . . But if you can gain your freedom, avail yourself of the opportunity.'' One principle is set over against another. Under certain conditions the first principle holds, while under other conditions the second takes precedence as the higher principle. This so often is the way with ethical decisions which Christians must make. Paul clearly teaches this scale of values in 1 Corinthians 7.

Except for an incidental reference in Romans 7:1–4, which we shall consider next, the remainder of the New Testament is silent on the question of divorce and remarriage. The legalistic declaration of Jesus is nowhere repeated or even alluded to. One thing is certain: neither Jesus nor Paul gave a complete teaching on the subject. If anything is clear from the contexts we have studied it is that they are all specific, not universal, save for the isolated statement of Jesus recorded in Luke, and the declaration of Jesus in the Sermon on the Mount. The one is a statement of God's absolute ethical design, the other is a part of the Kingdom mandate, the law of the coming Kingdom. We are left with the sense of a transition taking place, until the question of marital failure is like that of any other ethical failure in Christian experience; it is subject to God's grace expressed in realized forgiveness and renewal to life's highest possibilities again. From the words of Jesus we can draw an ideal, *not apply a law.* This leads not only to compassionate understanding of those who fail, but a supporting love which desires to see them restored by grace to the new possibilities God has in store. If sin has been a part of the marital failure, it must be confessed and repudiated so that a new experience may be entered with penitence and the desire for God's best.

All that we have studied of the words of Jesus and those of Paul, lead us to a question which presses for some kind of answer. In the context of a legal debate with the Pharisees in which the integrity of the Mosaic Law was at issue, Jesus allowed for divorce only under the condition of unchastity. He amplified this in His Kingdom teaching to reveal the higher demands of divine law when administered by the King in His Kingdom. A comparison of sayings shows that Jesus at times spoke the absolute will of God that makes no provision for divorce, for the marriage bond is intrinsically indissoluble. At other times He allowed divorce for an exception. The question now is what exceptions of a still different nature, such as would arise at other times, might also warrant the permission of divorce. We have no way of knowing, but the very fact that Jesus could cite the absolute ideal on one occasion, yet admit to an exception on another, and that Paul could do the same (and a different exception at that!), leads us to suppose that there is *a developing principle of excep-*

tions demonstrable in the New Testament. Divorce, under the
severity of the Old Testament law, was a redemptive recourse
which did not change the law of marriage, but released couples
from the application of the law in recognition of weakness and
inability. Is there not a similar principle at work in the New
Covenant of the age of grace? Does the Church experience less
grace or more in God's redemptive program for this time between the times?

The New Testament does not attempt to deal with all causes
of marital breakdown, but in 1 Corinthians 7:12–16 we have an
example of how the Church did deal with one such case.
Perhaps the Word of God is here demonstrating the principle of
adaptation. A general rule is held as the intention of God; this is
to be uncompromisingly declared, for it is God's righteous standard. But a grave necessity, an impossible situation imposed by
human failure, is then a matter of God's grace and the accommodation of His conditional will. Perhaps such a principle as
this would preclude the necessity of Paul's taking up all the possible cases which the churches might address to him. Perhaps
God is saying through all of this that there is a divinely ordained
norm; we are to think only of adhering to that—this is our commitment. But we live provisionally, knowing that human failure
is a reality of life—even among some choice Christian men and
women. The whole of the New Testament Epistles tells us in so
many ways that Christian life is lived, not under law but under
grace. Grace does not compromise God's norm; grace redeems
and restores those who fail to meet God's norm. Grace has the
final word; grace is triumphant!

Before we close this chapter, one further passage from the
Epistles must briefly be considered so that no New Testament
reference to divorce and remarriage shall have been left out.
This is the allusion to marriage in Romans 7:1–3:

> Do you not know, brethren—for I am speaking to those who
> know the law—that the law is binding on a person only during his
> life? Thus a married woman is bound by law to her husband as

long as he lives; but if her husband dies she is discharged from
the law concerning the husband. Accordingly, she will be called
an adulteress if she lives with another man while her husband is
alive. But if her husband dies she is free from that law, and if she
marries another man she is not an adulteress.

Really, the subject here is not marriage, but the nature of the
law. It is a theme continued from the previous chapter. Marriage
is brought in incidentally to illustrate the point being made. In
Romans 6 Paul taught that the death of Christ gives us deliverance from the law; we are henceforth free from it. By way of
illustration, Paul calls attention to the general law of marriage,
namely that a woman is bound to her husband by law so long as
he is alive. Paul is only concerned with the general law, not with
any possible exceptions. Thus, although Jesus allowed an exception for the cause of adultery, and Paul himself allowed an exception in the case of an unbelieving partner, no exceptions
whatever are mentioned here. Paul simply isn't concerned with
exceptions at all. His point is plain enough as it is. He makes no
mention of divorce, nor of the person whose remarriage comes
within the exception of unchastity. This is similar to what we
discovered in the Synoptic Gospels. Mark and Luke state the
general law which makes no mention of exceptions; Matthew
modifies that general law by declaring an exception. In neither
case is this contradictory; the purposes are different. One does
not need to mention any exceptions when declaring the nature of
the general law. As Archbishop R. C. Trench put it,
". . . nothing is proved by the absence of a doctrine from one
passage, which is clearly stated in others." So we glance at Romans 7:1–3, not to add anything to our understanding of the
New Testament teaching on divorce and remarriage, but merely
to note how the general law of marriage is employed as a Pauline
illustration of the strength of the law.

10

The Triumph of Grace

If anything should have been assimilated from our study to this point, it is that the rule of grace places the Christian under, not a new law, but an extraordinary ethical ideal. Such an ideal breaks through the wrappings of the sayings of Jesus in the Synoptic Gospels. Wherever His saying is in the form of an absolute, it becomes for the Christian an ideal framed in the form God intended it from the beginning. Wherever His saying is conditioned by an exception, it is proposed in its administrative form for the future Kingdom rule. Nonetheless, it is always more than that; it is God's righteous ideal, His pure intent, given to guide Christians in fulfilling the will of God insofar as they are able to appropriate the power of the Holy Spirit to do so. God does not compromise His ethical demand even when it is administered under His conditional will for Christians in the process of their becoming strong and mature. That ideal is always a judgment upon a Christian's actions, especially his failures. But it doesn't place him under condemnation—that is quite another thing. *Nor should it put him under the judgment of the Church!* This has been the case long enough, and this book calls for the boldness of grace to make a change. If the Church chooses to feel embarrassment over the conduct of its members, let it choose more likely targets—the inveterate gossips, the proud and pompous officeholders, the affluent who do not share their wealth with God's needy ones. Divorced persons have borne the office of the scapegoat long enough. The new embarrassment is that the Church cannot minister to the divorced in her midst because her theology of divorce and remarriage has been found wanting. Uneasy pastors readily confess this in pastors' workshops where the author frequently has been privileged to be in dialogue with them. There is indeed an uneasy conscience in the Church today. Is not the God of grace and compassion speaking? Have we ears to hear and hearts to respond? Or are we relieved that there is a group of God's people on whom the accumulated guilts of the Church can rest? Where else in all the sphere of human relationships may the healing, redemptive ministry of the Church be better displayed than among those whose intimate life has suffered dissolution?

We have lifted the words of Jesus to the place of an ethical ideal, and this calls for a final bit of examination. An ideal is indivisible and unexceptional, yet there are degrees of both success and failure in its attainment. The absolute nature of the ideal is unaffected by these degrees of success and failure in its attainment. What it demands is continual, responsible choice in life situations of conflict and human weakness. The ideals themselves are unceasing in their demand—absolutes standing as primary criteria for Christian value judgments and personal choices. When lost, an ideal can be regained. But a legal norm is lost in the breaking and cannot be regained. How fitting, then, that the age of grace is governed by ideals which are subject to God's full redemptive initiative! These ideals are regainable!

Jesus continues to insist upon the utmost reality of this ideal of marriage, since it alone will bring lasting happiness and the fulfillment of God's intention. But this still leaves us today as it left Matthew and Paul with problems of how to go on with life among weak human beings whose stages of Christian growth reflect so many possibilities of failure. For them it may be the ultimate question of how to preserve peace and life itself. The New Testament itself records two exceptions as its experience of life in Christ progressed, and before Christ is all in all, there will be many more exceptions where divorce and remarriage must be accepted as part of the pain and loss which accrues to human weakness and failure.

None of this, as should be perfectly evident, creates a casual attitude either toward marriage or divorce. In fact, it does just the opposite! Divorce is the destruction of that which God instituted for man's highest welfare and happiness. Yet, at the same time, divorce is a tragic example of the broken conditions which occasioned the redemption which Jesus embodies, and the areas of life that require His redemptive touch. As marital dissolution may display the fact of failure, so remarriage may display the fact of redemption. The Church has witnessed before the world to the redemption which brings salvation. It has so often witnessed to the power of God's grace to heal and restore, to redemptively touch broken areas of our lives. Is it not misfortune magnified that too often it has shrunk back from holding out the redemptive touch that can heal the hurt of divorce and rejoice with those who remarry with the vision of creating a truly Christian marriage?

For one of the most telling illustrations of grace in the New Testament, we must take up the New American Standard Bible, laying aside for the time the Revised Standard Version which has been our constant companion in this study. The reason for this is that ancient manuscripts do not all contain the familiar story found in the eighth chapter of John's Gospel, and the Revised Standard Version translators chose to delete it. It is a magnificent story and we are not inclined to debate the merits of its inclusion in the New Testament canon. Let us allow the Spirit of God to speak to us in an authentic voice.

A familiar situation greets us, for the first thing we read is: "And the scribes and the Pharisees brought a woman caught in adultery. . . . 'Now in the Law Moses commanded us to stone such women; what then do You say?' " (John 8:3–5 NAS). Once again Jesus is put to the test and made to interpret the law of

Moses. Little did these Pharisees realize that He was the very Author of the law, and its final interpreter.

The important observation to be made first is that here we have an actual encounter of Jesus with a case of proven adultery. The context is that of the Mosaic Law and the challenge of the Pharisees as to Jesus' true relation to it. As verse 6 clearly states, "And they were saying this, testing Him, in order that they might have grounds for accusing Him . . . ." And what is remarkable is that Jesus, in no sense opposed to the law and giving no teaching that would supersede it (such as in the Sermon on the Mount), gave them a direction which actually seemed to countenance the harsh penalty of the Mosaic Law. Yet the Lord of all grace was above the law which He had given, and the condition which He placed upon those who would execute the law changed everything. ". . . He who is without sin among you, let him be the first to throw a stone at her" (v. 7 NAS). We learn nothing new as to how Jesus regards the seriousness of adultery, for His law is absolute and uncompromised. What we do learn is how Jesus' response to failure is conditioned by grace. So what Jesus *does* stands in contrast with what Jesus *says*. And this is not of the nature of contradiction; it is the superseding nature of grace in the employment of the law's Author. And more than anything else this introduces us to the transition Jesus was even then making from the law, under which He had come, to the grace which was to rule in the Church Age.

What a change of scene in a brief few moments! ". . . and He was left alone, and the woman . . . in the midst" (v. 9 NAS). Every accusing voice had departed. Again Jesus speaks, ". . . Did no one condemn you? . . . Neither do I condemn you; go your way; from now on sin no more" (vv. 10, 11 NAS). How gracious is our Lord! How utterly different is His approach and solution—He who was the Author of the condemning law! Yet we must be careful to note that the reason He did not condemn

her was altogether different from the reason they did not. For
they could not carry out the condemnation of the law; they, too,
were guilty of sin. But Jesus was the one sinless person there;
He established her guilt by the law, established the procedure
for punishing her, and *He Himself was the sinless One who then
had the right, yes the duty, to throw the first stone!* But He did
not; He released her from the penalty with the word of forgiveness. He dealt with her in grace. Without compromising the law,
Jesus nonetheless was completely redemptive: *there was no
executed penalty!* What an opportunity for Jesus to have said,
"Now, of course, since you are indeed guilty of adultery, you
can never marry; you do understand this, don't you?" But quite
the contrary, Jesus was absolutely silent as to any further consequence of her sin. He forbade her nothing. Nor was He guilty
of forgetfulness or neglect! This is the towering majesty of the
Lord of all grace! Though He stood under the law, He was in
the shadow of the cross. He anticipated Calvary and acted in
that anticipation of the sacrifice that would enable Him to meet
every failure on the basis of grace alone. And the question to us
is a very simple one: Will the Church exemplify less grace than
the Lord Jesus Christ? Will we not understand that, while the
law is absolute, never compromised, and marriage is intrinsically indissoluble, there is the conditioned response of grace
which sets the failing ones free! Shall we not dare to err on the
side of realized forgiveness and the redemptive nature of grace
which creates new possibilities for fulfilling life's highest and
best, rather than to err on the side of the legalistic absolutes
which Jesus spoke in the context of the law?

If, in Matthew, Jesus is speaking a new law to the Church,
saying that a remarried person is guilty of adultery (even one
who looks upon a woman to lust after her is guilty of adultery!),
then what is the Church in its authoritative discipline to do in
such instances as may come before it? Should such ones be
stoned to death? Is there a new penalty given by Jesus to fit the

new law, if law it is? No! There is the same provision which suggests itself in the way Jesus the Lawgiver treated the guilty adulteress—the provision of grace, of forgiveness, of a new, fulfilled life not encumbered with legal sanctions. He acts as Redeemer, not as Lawgiver!

I like the official statement of the Presbyterian Church which was adopted in 1958: ". . . remarriage after a divorce granted on grounds explicitly stated in Scripture, or implicit in the gospel of Christ, may be sanctioned in keeping with His redemptive gospel, when sufficient penitence for sin and failure is evident, and a firm purpose of an endeavor after Christian marriage is manifest."

Whatever else it is, divorce is but the recognition and formal ending of a broken marriage. There is first the failure of a broken marriage vow—the actual death of marriage (if ever it was indeed a true marriage by biblical definition and standards). All divorce is failure; this is one reality which divorced persons —all divorced persons—must come to terms with. This does not mean, however, that divorce is a direct result of sin on the part of one or both partners. Of course, it may very well be and in all too many instances is, but not always. Divorce, like all human failures in the area of interpersonal relationships, is a consequence of the disorder which sin has brought into the world. The very mismatching of two persons that sometimes leads to total inability to merge two lives successfully, and that inevitably leads to divorce, may be attributed simply to human weakness which owes its origin to man's sinful and disabled state. But this cannot be construed to mean that all divorce is the consequence of particular sin or hardness of heart on the part of the persons involved. Nor does this mean that divorce can always be avoided, any more than other areas of life can be totally exempt from failure. This is not realism. And while it is impossible to judge one partner to be the "innocent party," can we not assume that there are instances where one party is for all responsible purposes the innocent party? Yet remarriage for him or her under the absolute law of Jesus is disallowed. What then? Are they objects of His grace or the absolute law? Pastors are faced with a decision here which they cannot escape making.

Even physical unfaithfulness, as every counselor knows so well, may only be the final expression of a marriage that has long since died. What divorce often signifies is that a formal marriage was not in any sense a true marriage according to the design of God. In so many instances it would be difficult if not impossible to say, "What God has joined together." There are marriages, well intended at the start, which never realize any semblance of the unity of persons envisioned by the biblical concept. *The failure is not the divorce; the failure was the marriage itself.* To perpetuate the marriage may be only to perpetuate a lie. And to make it more may be beyond the capacity of the individuals involved, despite their Christian orientation. Any pastoral expectation is sheer unreality in such cases, and indicates the need for pastoral self-examination.

The justification for remarriage in God's sight must arise from the reality of grace. Remarriage is always related to the renewing grace of God, which meets a person in his or her failure and grants another chance. This is not only true of the "innocent party," but the "guilty party" as well. For grace to be grace means that there is no intrinsic justification at all, no "right" which enters the picture to guide our evaluation and action. It is not a matter of personal right, but of God's grace in Christ. In this sense the title of this book is merely stated for the purpose of provoking the reader to come along and study, to be intrigued with the possibilities which hitherto have remained unexplored. But the right to remarry is neither a personal nor an absolute right at all; it is granted, not by the Creation orders, nor by the law of the Kingdom, but only by the grace of a forgiving Lord. It is neither *granted* for any cause, nor *not granted* for any cause; it is not related to cause at all. It is related only to grace. Thus it must be accompanied by penitence, no matter how guiltless the party may believe himself to be. Divorce and remarriage, however warranted by circumstances, is still antithetical to the Creation order, to the ethical absolute. Innocent and guilty alike are denied a case "for cause." But all alike are invited to come in penitence, to confess whatever sin may have been involved, and to apply to God's unlimited grace in Christ Jesus. All is renewable in God's grace.

The uniqueness of Christ was His appeal to an absolute ethic (every dissolved marriage violates the ethical order of God, and is ethical adultery), and His gift of realized forgiveness and renewal to life's highest and best possibilities. The true spirit of Christ is neither a compromise of the divine ethic, nor of a justifiable human failure. It is a nonlegalistic accommodation of God on the principle of grace alone, transcending every other consideration. This removes all remarriage from the question of who is right and who is wrong, which remarriage is valid and which is not; these are but legal questions belonging to the Mosaic or Kingdom Law. Remarriage is a question of grace, and of nothing more.

Dr. Ray S. Anderson, esteemed colleague whose insights have distilled into my own, says it so well: "If the church is such a thing as grace, then let the church be bold in grace. The stigmas that the church places upon those who bear the marks of sin have no existence in the sight of Christ." Yes, having been admitted to the Church of *grace,* let us be bold in grace! This is the distinguishing feature of all the New Testament Epistles which are exclusively directed to the life of the Church.

Do we then ignore and repudiate the words of Jesus in His Kingdom mandate? God forbid! The ethic of the coming Kingdom shines as a guiding light upon the Christian's path. It declares the righteousness of God in absolute terms, perceiving failure in legal terms and in the manner in which it shall be administered under the rule of the King in His glorious reign on earth. But the secondary purpose it serves is to illumine the Christian mind and challenge the Christian will as to God's pure intention. The decisive feature, however, is that it does not place the failing Christian under the condemning status of a broken law. It does not deal with failure in terms of penalty.

A recent study seeks to promote the idea that there is a principle of tolerance under which God works out His compassion. Nothing could be further from the truth! Tolerance, like leniency, precludes grace and forgiveness, as Paul Tournier carefully points out. Tolerance or leniency is a way of overlooking the true nature of the failure, as though it were not a serious thing in the eyes of God. But divorce always is a serious thing in the eyes of God; this cannot be glossed over by tolerance or leniency. To merely be tolerant would preclude the possibility of God's revealing the tragic nature of all that led to the divorce, of His disclosing the true consequences of violating the ethical design of God, and then His going on from there to grant full forgiveness by grace. No tolerance, no justification, no human right can be allowed to stand between the divorced person and the grace of God. It all reduces to this.

Remarriage for some may be a redemptive fulfillment, a new opportunity to reverse the former failure, to fulfill the order of Creation in a particular marriage, to seek an enduring, Christ-controlled marriage. Where divorce has been judged necessary for the well-being of the parties involved, the divorced person may enter a marriage so centered in Christ's love and purpose that any divorce of that marriage would be impossible. In a renewed opportunity, such a spiritually motivated person will demonstrate the intrinsically indissoluble nature of a truly Christian marriage—and this to the glory of God. Remarriage can be redemptive!

For the pastor who seeks to adapt a marriage ceremony for the remarriage of divorced persons, a suggested portion might read as follows:

And they have, in my presence, expressed before God a genuine penitence for such elements of their past marital relationship as call for penitence, submitting themselves to God's forgiving and liberating grace, and have prayed to Him for renewal in their dedication to the common life which they now resolve by faith to establish together. They are here taking that step of faith in the re-creating power of God and in His care for their mutual good.

Let the Church be bold in grace! Let the divorced and remarried feel fully accepted in the community of sinners saved by grace! Let the remarried find places of service in the Church alongside those whose experience of the forgiving grace of God concerns less conspicuous areas of life. Let there be no penalties in the Church where God disallows such penalties. Let there be a recognition of the necessity for the tragic moral choice in this world, the necessity, at times, of choosing the lesser of two evils. Let us rejoice that the absolute will of God is not compromised, but that He conditions the exercise of His will to our imperfect faith and obedience, to our sins and our failures. And may the knowledge of such great grace fill our minds and hearts with such responding love as will motivate us to attempt in every way to fulfill His highest will in the power of enabling grace!

Hastings Rashdall, years ago, had a good word with which we can close: "That the ideal is permanent monogamous marriage is undoubtedly the principle which Jesus taught . . . . By what detailed enactments, however, the ideal may be best promoted, and which is the less of two evils when that ideal has been violated and made impossible, is a question which must be settled by the moral consciousness, the experience, and the practical judgment of the present. And no one branch of Christendom, we may add, has a monopoly of the Christian conscience in this matter."

As the divorce law in the Old Testament was a concession to human weakness and failure, so New Testament grace allows for the same. It is never God's pure intention that marriage be dissolved, but it is never God's intention that some marriages be formed and continue as they are, either. So divorce and remarriage come within His conditional will for this age. So, too, while divorce and remarriage are not allowed within the law of Christ's Kingdom save for the single cause of adultery, they are permitted by the grace of Christ, the Lord of the Church. While not specifically taught in the direct words of Jesus, the order of necessity is recognized in the larger ethical context of the New Testament. And what is permissible in the larger context of New Testament ethics must be permissible in the pastoral ministry of the Church. There must be a positive affirmation that divorce and remarriage are sometimes redemptive means, fully within the present will of God. Unhesitatingly, though always sadly, the Christian can affirm: "I believe in divorce and remarriage—*sometimes.*"

Bibliography

Amram, David W. *The Jewish Law of Divorce According to the Bible and the Talmud*. New York: Hermon Press, 1968.

Barclay, William. *The Gospel of Matthew*. Philadelphia: The Westminster Press, 1957.

Barrett, C. K. *A Commentary on the First Epistle to the Corinthians*. New York: Harper & Row, 1968.

Bassett, William W., ed. *The Bond of Marriage: An Ecumenical and Interdisciplinary Study*. Notre Dame: Univ. of Notre Dame Press, 1968.

Bright, John. *The Kingdom of God*. Nashville: Abingdon, 1953.

Brown, Raymond E. *The Gospel According to John*. The Anchor Bible. Garden City: Doubleday, 1966.

Bruce, F. F. *Commentary on the Book of Acts*. Grand Rapids: Eerdmans, 1954.

Chafer, Lewis Sperry. *Grace*. Philadelphia: The Sunday School Times Co., 1922.

————. *Systematic Theology*. Dallas: Dallas Theological Seminary Press, 1947.

Dibelius, Martin. *The Sermon on the Mount*. New York: Scribners, 1940.

Duty, Guy. *Divorce and Remarriage*. Minneapolis: Bethany Fellowship, 1967.

Emerson, James, Jr. *Divorce, the Church, and Remarriage*. Philadelphia: Westminster Press, 1961.

Epstein, Louis M. *Marriage Laws in the Bible and the Talmud*. Cambridge: Harvard Univ. Press, 1942.

Grosheide, F. W. *Commentary on the First Epistle to the Corinthians*. Grand Rapids: Eerdmans, 1953.

Ladd, George Eldon. *A Theology of the New Testament*. Grand Rapids: William B. Eerdmans, 1974.

―――. *Jesus and the Kingdom*. New York: Harper & Row, 1964.

McArthur, Harvey K. *Understanding the Sermon on the Mount*. New York: Harper & Row, 1960.

McClain, Alva. *The Greatness of the Kingdom*. Grand Rapids: Zondervan, 1959.

Morris, Leon. *The First Epistle of Paul to the Corinthians*. London: The Tyndale Press, 1958.

Murray, John. *Divorce*. Philadelphia: The Committee on Christian Education, The Orthodox Presbyterian Church, 1953.

Ramsey, Paul and Outka, Gene H. *Norm and Context in Christian Ethics*. New York: Charles Scribners Sons, 1968.

Thielicke, Helmut. *Theological Ethics*. Vol. I. Foundations. ed. by William H. Lazareth. Philadelphia: Fortress Press, 1966.

―――. *The Ethics of Sex*. New York: Harper & Row, 1964.

Windisch, Hans. *The Meaning of the Sermon on the Mount*. Eng. trans. by S. M. Gilmour. Philadelphia: Westminster Press, 1951.